# THE SOCIOLOGY
# OF THE MEAL

ROY C. WOOD

**EDINBURGH UNIVERSITY PRESS**

*For James and Elizabeth Steel*

© Roy C. Wood, 1995

Edinburgh University Press Ltd
22 George Square, Edinburgh

Typeset in Palatino
by Pioneer Associates Ltd, Perthshire, and
printed and bound in Great Britain by
The Alden Press, Oxford

A CIP record for this book is available
from the British Library

ISBN 0 7486 0596 7

# Contents

# Acknowledgements

Many people offered intellectual, moral and practical support during the writing of this book. I owe several intellectual debts to my friend and former colleague Dr James Steel, who opened my eyes to many aspects of eating behaviour that would have otherwise remained a mystery to me. Over a number of years, my association with Cailein Gillespie, Peter Cullen and Dr Michael Riley – good companions all – has provided many opportunities for fruitful debate and reflection. More recently, Joseph Fattorini's unique approach to personal and professional comradeship has proved helpful in clarifying my own thoughts on certain topics germane to the content of this text. I have similarly benefited from the friendship, support and encouragement of Arnaud Frapin-Beaugé, Donald Sloan and Mona Clark. Finally, I owe an unrepayable debt to my colleagues Jean Finlayson and Sandra Miller, whose diverse skills eased the production of the manuscript and brought it to a manageable whole. As always, errors of judgement, taste and fact are those of the author alone.

Glasgow, June 1994

# 1

---

# Food and Social Theory:
## States of the Art

---

This book is a sociological study of the role of meals in (predominantly British) society. The terms 'sociology' and 'sociological' are used in the broadest sense, to indicate a focus upon social behaviour with respect to food and, at a formal academic level, to acknowledge that the discussion contained within this text draws upon concepts from a number of academic disciplines, including most notably, social anthropology. There is a purpose to this interpretative strategy. To say that sociologists have come late to the study of food and eating is, judging by the frequent repetition of the sentiment in recent commentaries, to articulate a near-truism. To talk of the 'sociology of food and eating' is, in effect, to talk of the social anthropology and sociology of food and eating, for it is in the former discipline that the systematic study of cultural dimensions to food consumption has its intellectual origins (Murcott, 1988). The relatively recent interest in food shown by sociologists has, perhaps, blurred this point, as active researchers and writers have appropriated and synthesised much early scholarship, gathering it under the sociological umbrella in an effort to consolidate, analyse and advance understanding of food-culture relationships.

Accordingly, it makes good sense to recognise that a broad definition of the sociological is appropriate to the study of food and eating, as it is not sensible to ignore relevant broader intellectual themes and concepts drawn from other areas of academic inquiry. A related reason for adopting an eclectic approach lies in the nature of sociology itself. Sociology is a curious phenomenon in the sense that, while its practitioners make claims to disciplinary status, sociology has few apparent boundaries in terms of what its practitioners study, and very little distinctiveness beyond what these practitioners claim as legitimate objects of inquiry. The essential fluidity of sociology as a discipline is captured in a comprehensive work of reference by Jary and Jary, who write that 'no aspect of society is excluded from consideration by sociology, no simple distinction can be drawn between sociology and social science; in some usages the two terms are simply synonymous' (1991: 603). They go on to remark that 'sociology does not exist as a tightly integrated discipline; not only does the subject encompass many competing paradigms and approaches, it has also remained uniquely open to ideas imported from other disciplines . . .' (ibid.).

The last observation is entirely true of the sociological study of food and eating. There can be no disagreement over the claim that social *scientific* interest in food and eating has generated a substantial literature. Murcott attributes the bulk of contributions to 'social anthropologists, social historians, social nutritionists so-called and other social commentators' (1983b: 1). A broad interpretation of what constitutes the 'sociological' is thus appropriate to the study of the social aspects of diet and, if this point seems somewhat laboured, it is only because of the related observation that it remains something of a difficulty to identify precisely a distinctive *sociology* of food and eating. Put another way, it is not unreasonable to assert that sociologists have yet to find their own, particular, 'voice' in this area of social inquiry, a voice that goes beyond simply linking the discipline's own traditional concerns to the study of food and eating – namely a preoccupation with modern, Western, industrial societies and with forms of social structure and inequality (for example, the structure and inequality of class, gender and ethnic relations).

These are, of course, important issues, and sociological investigation of food habits has extended much historical and social anthropological research by elaborating areas of interest often ignored by those disciplines' practitioners. However, the case must not be exaggerated, for across all the social science disciplines the total number of researchers actively engaged in analysis of the cultural aspects of diet remains small. This reflects in part the taken-for-granted nature of diet-culture relationships which, for many academic analysts, are regarded as being at the margins of individual disciplinary concerns. A fair proportion of the empirical literature to emerge as a result of sociologists' interest in food and eating has been the by-product of other research programmes, where exploration of the cultural dimensions to diet was not a major, or even original, research objective. Greater consistency and more directed empirical research is promised in the UK as projects sponsored by the Economic and Social Research Council's initiative 'The Nation's Diet: the Social Science of Food Choice' come to fruition. To date, however, the greatest synergy in sociological work on food and eating has been in the area of theoretical development and synthesis, in the efforts of sociologists to construct frameworks that comfortably accommodate often disparate research findings and traditions, and theoretical perspectives. For a relatively underdeveloped specialist research area within the social sciences, a considerable degree of theoretical pluralism exists in approaches to the study of food and eating, and any study of the field must take cognisance of this theoretical pluralism. Accordingly, the remainder of this chapter is devoted to analysing the key themes and issues raised so far in theoretical debate.

THEORETICAL ORIENTATIONS

No assessment of the varieties of social scientific theoretical perspectives on food and eating can fail to take account of the ready-made framework for such analysis provided by Murcott (1988) and subsequently modified in Mennell, Murcott and van Otterloo (1992). In her article, Murcott reviews sociological and social anthropological approaches to food and eating and distinguishes between 'structural' and 'materialist' perspectives on the topic. In essence, she argues, key theorists in the field have worked from within one of these broad but distinctive intellectual traditions. The key structural writers are identified as the social anthropologists Claude Lévi-Strauss and Mary Douglas. The major materialist writers are the social anthropologists Marvin Harris and Jack Goody, the political scientist and historian Sidney Mintz, and the sociologist Stephen Mennell. In her collection with the last-named of these writers and Anneke van Otterloo (1992), Murcott's framework has been modified somewhat, evidently in cooperation with her co-authors. The term 'structural' has been abandoned in favour of 'structuralism', and 'materialist' has become 'developmentalism'. The number of writers embraced by the first label has also increased and includes the French sociologists Pierre Bourdieu and Claude Fischler.

Murcott (1988) uses the term 'structural' to embrace the work of a number of writers the majority of whom would conventionally be labelled structuralists, the term subsequently adopted in her later collaborative work (Mennell, Murcott and van Otterloo, 1992). Her preference in this choice of terminology is based on the observation that some of the writers brought within this boundary would not regard themselves as structuralists, or be classified as such by other commentators. Relatedly, structuralism itself, like so many kinds of social theory, does not represent a coherent, unified series of perspectives on the social world. There may not be as many structuralists as there are structuralisms, but in marketing terms the latter are well differentiated into distinctive brands. In the most general sense, all social scientists are to some degree engaged in structural analysis, concerned to ascertain the crucial patterns or shapes of cultural phenomena, social groupings and social activities (Bottomore and Nisbet, 1979: 557). However, in contemporary social theory, structuralism has come to have more limited and specific connotations as an approach to analysis originating in the work of French intellectuals such as Claude Lévi-Strauss, Roland Barthes (a literary critic), Michel Foucault (a philosopher and historian of ideas) and Louis Althusser (a Marxist political scientist). (For a detailed discussion of the origins and development of structuralism, see Sturrock, 1986.)

Insofar as it is possible to distinguish the central tenet of structuralism, it is that societies, social institutions and social action can be analysed in a manner analogous with language, as structures of often unobservable meaning that can nevertheless be detected in the relationships that exist between elements in the 'language'. In this specific though still pluralistic form, structuralism is concerned to treat cultural phenomena as elements in systems of signs and symbols. The relationships between these elements, their patterning, are the concern of the structuralist. Typically, structuralists talk in terms of 'codes' and 'ciphers' when referring to these patterns, which are seen as taking on regular forms like hierarchy, opposition, contrast, close association and so on. Thus, in the realm of food, Julia Twigg (1983) has analysed the dominant meat-eating culture and suggested a hierarchy of food at the apex of which is red meat. This is followed, in descending order, by less bloody and white meats, fish and fowl, eggs and cheese, and finally vegetables and fruit. Lévi-Strauss, as will be shown later, is interested in oppositions between different states of food and types of cooking. Roland Barthes analyses close associations between certain foodstuffs (for example, steak and chips) and between these foodstuffs and emotions and other qualities such as strength and virility.

Structuralists then see the cultural significance of natural and social phenomena as deriving from the relationships among such phenomena, relationships which are normally established by convention as a result of human social action: such phenomena 'signify' meaning to social actors, and such meaning is mutable. For example, Barthes (1973) argues that wine signifies different things in different cultures: in France it can be seen as refreshing, in England as creating dehydration and drowsiness. Meaning may also change over time as the values attached to national and cultural phenomena change, a point demonstrated for the case of sugar by Mintz (1985). At the risk of oversimplification therefore, structuralism, in Culler's words, 'takes from linguistics two cardinal principles: that signifying entities do not have essences [intrinsic meanings] but are defined by networks of relations, both internal and external, and that to account for signifying phenomena is to describe the system of norms that make them possible' (Culler, 1983: 79).

Turning now to what Murcott (1988) described as 'materialist' approaches to the sociological study of food and eating and what, in the later reworking of her framework for understanding theoretical contributions to the field, has become 'developmentalism' (Mennell, Murcott and van Otterloo, 1992), an immediate semantic difficulty must be encountered. As previously noted, the materialist approach embraces the work of social anthropologists (Harris, Goody), the sociologist Mennell and the political scientist Sidney Mintz. The term 'materialist' is, as Mennell, Murcott and van Otterloo (1992) note, one that Harris would adopt, but is too specific for the other writers. Indeed, in this volume, Mennell is reported as objecting to the term as originally used by Murcott (1988), by this time his co-author, in favour of the label 'developmentalist'. This then accounts for the change in terminology. It is probably a sensible choice except for the case of Harris who, as Murcott notes in her earlier report, 'sidesteps study of historical development and changes over time' (1988: 20). Developmentalism is concerned with the historical evolution of food practices and preferences. While accepting – if only half-heartedly – structuralists' concerns with patterns of symbolic meaning, developmentalist writers are more concerned to demonstrate how understanding of contemporary food habits is improved through the examination of historical trends and data. Structuralists are depicted as too concerned with the 'here and now' and their analyses usually castigated for being incomplete and largely idealist, ignoring the biological imperatives underlying food habits (the need to eat to live) and the array of biological, geographical and technological factors that influence food supply, understanding of which is seen as a necessary precursor to any analysis of abstract 'symbolic' associations attached to food within a given social context.

THEORETICAL CONTRIBUTIONS

The objective of this section is to discuss the work of some of the key writers in both structuralist and developmentalist traditions. Like a general understanding of these theoretical orientations, this exercise is necessary to an informed perspective on the sociological study of food and eating and to an understanding of the sociology of meals. It also requires a degree of selectivity. Both the reviews of Murcott (1988) and Mennell, Murcott and van Otterloo (1992) cover a range of authors in varying depth, and it is the objective here to avoid simply aping these and other, more specific, commentaries on particular writers (see for example, Passariello (1990) on Douglas, and Gofton (1986) on Bourdieu). Clearly, some overlap will be unavoidable. It is also necessary to note at the outset that several of the writers included in the undoubtedly carefully-wrought framework of Murcott are significant to theoretical understanding in the sociology of food and eating largely on the strength of one published work. This is to a great extent true of writers like Bourdieu and Goody, and to only a slightly lesser extent of

Mintz and Mennell. While the writings of all these authors are relevant to general theoretical development in the field, some are undoubtedly more important than others. So, of the four mentioned above, it is the contribution of Mennell which is outstanding. In the same context, the work of Roland Barthes attracts relatively little attention in most reviews, and his contribution is arguably underestimated. Furthermore, many of these theorists are in the main unconcerned about the explicit role of meals in society, a category into which Mennell, for example, would undoubtedly fall.

In what follows, an attempt has therefore been made to balance consideration of the work of those writers whose contribution to general theoretical development in the area cannot be ignored (for example, Harris and Mennell) and those whose work has some relevance for the present text's core theme. The result of this approach is that some writers are treated rather cursorily (for example, Lévi-Strauss and Goody) while others are afforded greater consideration (for example, Barthes, Elias and Mennell). Similarly, the centrality of Mary Douglas's work to the sociological analysis of the meal means that only the general orientation of her work is charted at this point. Two writers present in the Murcott (1988) and Mennell, Murcott and van Otterloo (1992) review framework are excluded entirely. The work of Sidney Mintz is not unimportant but his general theoretical concerns are very diffuse, ironically because his key analysis in the present context is highly focused in the study of one particular commodity, namely sugar. Also, as Murcott (1988) has observed, his position is very close to that of Harris.

While the exclusion of Mintz is to a degree a matter of expediency, detailed consideration of the work of Claude Fischler is excluded for different reasons. The all-too-easy tendency to seek to be comprehensive in accounting for theoretical pluralism in the study of an area like the sociology of food and eating cannot disguise the fact that, while a structuralist, much of Fischler's theoretical work is, like the present discussion, a commentary on different theoretical perspectives. In the view of Mennell, Murcott and van Otterloo (1992), this has led Fischler to argue that 'The very codes or structures governing eating habits that the structuralists pursued have, since the 1960s particularly, been undergoing a process of "destructuration"' (1992: 13), with the consequence that Fischler's theoretical position has converged with 'the more developmental perspectives emerging in Anglo-Saxon sociology . . .' (ibid.). A close reading of Fischler's work (for example, Fischler, 1980; 1988a) leaves nagging doubts as to whether he is quite the convert to the developmentalist cause that Mennell, Murcott and van Otterloo maintain. More important, however, is the observation that, in the field of writers active in research into the sociology of food and eating, Fischler's position is more akin to that of Murcott's own.

Murcott's contribution to the elaboration of both theoretical and empirical issues in the sociology of food and eating has been substantial (see, for example, Murcott, 1982; 1983a; 1983b; 1986a), and it is not inaccurate to describe her as the most consistently prolific British sociologist writing in the area during the 1980s. In her early study of the social significance of the cooked dinner in South Wales (examined further in Chapter 2), Murcott took a broadly structural approach to her work, the significance of which will become clearer shortly. Her later work has evidenced both a great versatility in exploring the cultural dimensions to food and eating from a variety of sociological and social policy standpoints, and a general absence of theoretical didacticism. Fischler, like Murcott, has made varied contributions of both an empirical and a theoretical nature to the sociological study of food and eating, mainly with a structuralist flavour. If not actually a convert to the developmentalist cause, there is, as with Murcott, some ambiguity as to his preferred theoretical position which reveals a tendency towards pragmatism and issue- rather than theory-oriented research (though on this account it should be said at once that Murcott has a considerable edge in both the range and sophistication of topics chosen for research). The 'commentator' aspect of Fischler's work will be returned to later in the chapter, and certain of his other contributions to the field will be touched upon at various points in the text.

### Claude Lévi-Strauss

Lévi-Strauss (1965) is generally regarded as the principal author of contemporary academic interest in food and eating. In a large body of work, it is undoubtedly Lévi-Strauss's concept of the culinary triangle that has attracted most attention.

Lévi-Strauss is concerned with the universal characteristics of the human species and in particular that feature unique to humans, the fact that they are products of both 'nature' and 'culture'; of nature because humans are animals, and of culture because humans have language and intelligence which form the basis for the construction of culture (Murcott, 1988). The 'universalist' in Lévi-Strauss leads him to the view that knowledge of the nature-culture composition of humankind is itself a ubiquitous feature of self-awareness in all societies, and to a degree, a source of tension that leads to cultural conflicts reflecting human perceptions of nature and the natural in an effort to resolve such tensions. Influenced like so many structuralists by structural linguistics, Lévi-Strauss takes the binary opposition of phonemes as the basis for many of his analyses (phonemes constitute the elements of meaning in language and are constructed from the oppositional qualities of contrasting phonetic sounds – see Sturrock, 1986: 39–57 for a detailed elaboration of this issue).

The linguistic concept of binary oppositions supposedly mirrors the opposition between nature and culture, and such oppositions form the basis for cultural constructs. Objects of culture are created in a manner which reflects human perceptions of nature. A clarification of this idea in the context of Lévi Strauss's work is offered by Leach (1974) in his example of how traffic lights (a cultural construct) relate to human perceptions of colour in nature. The colour spectrum, Leach argues, is a continuum, not a tapestry of discrete colours. Perceptually, however, the human mind tends to separate things into named classes, and when cultural artefacts are constructed they reflect these perceptions of nature. The human mind separates the colour spectrum into different colours, and people can be taught to feel that certain colours have particular values relative to each other. This is especially so of oppositional values such as red (danger/stop) and green (safe/go). These oppositions form the basis of the traffic signal. The third colour of the three-colour traffic signal – yellow – has been selected, Leach argues, because it lies midway between red and green in the colour spectrum, and because the desire for a third element is based on the perceived need for an intermediate signal between red and green. Thus, the red-yellow-green traffic signal, meaning stop-caution-go, is structurally a cultural phenomenon that reflects perceptions of nature – the instructions, or cultural element, are a transformation of the natural element – colours.

Leach says very little about how or why people can be (or are) taught to attribute meaning to such perceptions of nature. Lévi-Strauss is a little clearer in this respect. His culinary triangle is based on the proposition that most societies cook, and cooking is a process that transforms raw ingredients into cooked ones. Cooking is, as it were, a cultural transformation of nature. The binary opposition between the cooked and the raw is only one such relationship involved in the culinary triangle, for raw food can itself be transformed by nature if it is allowed to go off, to rot. The culinary triangle comprises this pair of binary oppositions (see Figure 1.1). The rotten is a natural transformation (elaboration) of both cooked and raw food, whereas cooked food is a cultural transformation of the raw. Just as with Leach's traffic-light example, the basic culinary triangle, Lévi-Strauss claims, maps the essential techniques of cooking – roasting, smoking and boiling. Thus, when food is roasted, it (a) requires minimal equipment (cultural objects); and (b) is brought into more or less direct contact with the agent of conversion, fire. In terms of process and product, roasting belongs to nature (though midway between on Lévi-Strauss' continuum, a fact that might be explained by the observation that roast food is always only partly cooked). Smoking, too, is a natural process, but smoked food (the product) 'belongs' to culture. This is because smoking preserves food, making it durable and, among other things, increasing its potential economic value. The process of smoking food (allegedly) requires no cultural apparatus but it does require air, unlike roasting where the contact between the agent of conversion (fire) and the material to be cooked is direct. Boiling is a process which reduces food to a state similar to that of rotted food in nature, so boiled food (the product) belongs to nature, but the process of boiling, requiring a receptacle (a cultural object), belongs to culture.

This then is the developed 'prototype' culinary triangle (Lévi-Strauss offers further developments, as does Lehrer, 1969; 1972). Figure 1.2 shows the transformation of states of food into cooking techniques. Leach remarks that 'readers might begin to suspect that the whole argument was an elaborate academic joke' (1974: 31). Mennell (1985: 9) suggests that the 'general reader may well consider the culinary triangle a farrago of nonsense'. The simplistic manner in which the culinary triangle is presented does not inspire confidence. What Lévi-Strauss is getting at is that structures like the culinary triangle can be used to analyse social behaviour across a range of societies because the principles of binary opposition uncovered in a particular cultural context, such as cooking, are intimations of universally shared mentalistic structures.

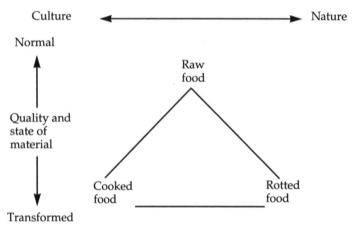

FIGURE 1.1 Basic culinary triangle after Lévi-Strauss (1965).

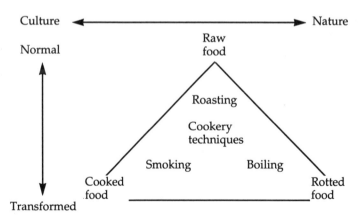

FIGURE 1.2 Developed culinary triangle after Lévi-Strauss (1965).

If Lévi-Strauss is correct, then the culinary triangle is a universal perceptual field and the basis for cooking techniques and hence recipes in all societies. Criticisms of this view of the universality of mentalistic structures range from a denial of the existence of sufficient empirical evidence to support the assertion, to doubts over Lévi-Strauss's methodology, especially the relevance or otherwise of the use of binary oppositions to analyse cultural phenomena. The culinary triangle is only one element of Lévi-Strauss's work on food, but it is the one that has captured the imagination and is important in the sociology of food and eating if only because other writers have reacted against it.

### *Mary Douglas*

Nowhere is the use of the term 'structural' rather than 'structuralist' (Murcott, 1988) more relevant than in the case of Mary Douglas. Douglas's writings have shown a preoccupation with structure that, while emphasising the symbolic, rarely engages in any great depth with the work of more avowedly structuralist writers like Lévi-Strauss and Barthes. In terms of the definitions discussed earlier, Douglas lies somewhere between the general structural approach to social analysis and the more vociferous structuralists. Her special importance to the present study lies, as previously noted, in her work on the sociology of the meal, examined further in Chapter 2. A general sketch of her theoretical orientations is, however, appropriate at this juncture.

As one of the key thinkers of late twentieth-century social anthropology, Douglas's work has been subject to extensive review in terms of her contribution to the study of food and eating (see Passariello, 1990). Her work on food is, at the theoretical and methodological level, motivated by a rejection of the universalist prescriptions of Lévi-Strauss's structuralism (Douglas, 1975). She is emphatic that the social analysis of food behaviours must be a 'bottom-up' rather than 'top-down' exercise, by which she means to argue for micro-sociological studies of food-culture relationships as a basis for building a bigger picture. 'The meanings of food', Douglas writes, 'need to be studied in small-scale exemplars. Attempts to generalize by using linguistic theoretical assumptions tend to produce explanations of tastes and preferences that seem too trivial or too bizarre' (Douglas, 1984: 8).

Douglas's structural(ist) credentials are articulated in her view that food is a symbolic system of communication but not the only symbolic system of communication. She is struck by the extent to which everyday life is highly ordered (or structured) and this order permeates all social activities, for example, care of the body and the choice and maintenance of clothing. These too are systems of communication and are linked with others – such as food systems. She argues that no particular manifestation of people's methods of ordering their lives can be isolated from any other. Thus, she notes, 'Food is . . . the medium through which a system of relationships within the family is expressed. Food is both a social matter and part of the provision for care of the body. Instead of isolating the food system, it is instructive to consider it frankly as one of a number of family body systems' (1982a: 86). In Douglas's terms then, food is an expressive, communicative system which reflects relationships within social groups such as families as well as people's attitudes to their bodies in terms of what is or is not regarded as acceptable/unacceptable and dangerous/not dangerous.

Douglas's published work on food and eating evidences both consistency and diversity in the range of topics studied. Recurring themes include preoccupation with the aesthetic qualities of food (1982b), and the modelling of components of the food system whether using computational methods (Douglas and Gross, 1981) or grid-group analysis (the precursor of which is indirectly mooted as early as 1973 but extended much later – see Douglas, 1982d). Douglas's work has always engendered controversy, and not only among academics. Her early, seminal, report on family meals was commissioned and sponsored by the UK Government's Department of Health and Social Security (Douglas, 1982a) and aroused some ire in Parliament (see Passariello, 1990). In this research project, Douglas's assistant, Nicod, stayed as a lodger in four working-class households for various short periods in order to study dietary consumption patterns. A flavour of the academic criticisms marshalled against Douglas's work is to be found in a review by Charsley. That each of the households studied by Douglas and Nicod had a family food system is, Charsley accepts, uncontentious. But, he continues, 'Because a single pattern could be identified in these four cases and appeared to be quite general in the streets in which they lived, Douglas moves on to ascribe it to the working class as a whole. A further small step makes it the British food system' (1992: 2). For Charsley, this is a dubious form of progressive generalisation. Indeed it is, and it is also not an entirely accurate representation of Douglas's arguments. For example, while her use of language is in many cases ambiguous, or certainly less than precise, Douglas clearly recognises differences within the national food system based on class (and, to a much lesser extent, gender).

This short discussion of Douglas's work has somewhat advanced before the argument. The rationale for this is simple. Much debate in the sociology of food gives the appearance of being torn between concern with detail, and discussion about the doubtfulness of being able to generalise such detail satisfactorily. Thus, Lévi-Strauss's theoretical universalism leads him to make grandiose empirical assertions, many of which are untenable. Douglas's micro-sociological empirical approach leaves her (in the view of many, at least) vulnerable to breathless theoretical generalisation. However, as will be shown later, developmental writers face similar problems.

### Roland Barthes

If Douglas is a 'general' structuralist, then Barthes belongs to the full-blooded kind, many of whose writings on the sociology of food predate those of most of the authors considered here (Barthes, 1973; 1979 ). Arguably, the most important of these is Barthes's essay 'Towards a psychosociology of contemporary food consumption' (1979) in which he argues, like Douglas after him, that food is a system of communication. To discover the constituents of the system, it is necessary to create an inventory of food products, techniques and habits, and from this observe patterns of signification.

The use of the term 'signification' in this context refers, of course, to the linguistic models of culture so favoured by structuralists. For Barthes, food signifies cultural meanings to those who consume it. Not all varieties of a foodstuff are necessarily significant at a collective social level: some are significant only as a reflection of personal taste. This distinction, allowing for the accommodation of individual food preferences and tastes (and their associated personal meanings) within a system of related general meanings attached to certain foods, permits construction of a 'grammar' of the most important foods in a given social setting. In seeking to allow for individual, psychological taste preferences within a coherent societal pattern of meanings attached to food, Barthes argues that foods alone rarely signify anything. Rather, it is the subdivisions of general food categories and the preparation of food and the uses to which it is put that create meaning. Though Barthes himself makes no such claim, it is not unreasonable to infer from this that apparently individual food preferences, even where they appear exceptional to some wider, consistent social patterning, are still the product to some degree of that patterning, for very few foods exist in a state of natural grace (somewhat dubiously, salmon, caviar and truffles are cited by Barthes as exceptions), and both individual and collective meanings and tastes are the outcome of human agency in the form of processes of selection, preparation and consumption.

Having said this, there can be little doubt that Barthes is more interested in the social rather than individual aspects of food tastes and preferences. He notes that food preferences vary according to social class: for example, sweet chocolate is preferred by the lower classes, bitter chocolate by the upper classes (in the then French cultural context). Furthermore, in seeking to elaborate a grammar of foods, Barthes concerns himself with the wider role of signification, of what purposes are served at the societal level by the shared meanings attendant on the selection, preparation and consumption of food. To this end, he turns to food advertising as a means of eliciting these shared meanings, arguing that food advertising reveals three thematic groups of shared meaning about food.

The first group of themes concern the historical. For Barthes, food has properties that allow people to have daily involvement in their national past. A second group of themes highlights the feelings of inferiority/superiority that may be attached to certain foods, 'superior' foods being aspired to and 'inferior' foods being abstained from for reasons of their status attributes. The final set of themes centres on the concept of health, often emphasising the 'traditional' health values of certain foods. Barthes concludes by pointing out that in France, 'food is becoming incorporated into an ever-lengthening list of situations' (1979: 172). Food signifies the situation in which it is used and 'has a constant tendency to transfer itself into situation' (ibid.). What Barthes appears to mean by this is that advertising can attach mythologies to certain foods that contradict and sometimes supplant traditional or scientific concepts of what these foods 'stand for'. For example, coffee, once considered a stimulant, is now advertised in such a way as to be associated with rest and relaxation (though the stimulatory effects of coffee are not denied). Barthes sees such transformations as leading to a state whereby food loses substance and gains in function, an assertion which is characteristically oblique but appears to suggest that the physical form of food has become less important than what it signifies.

Taken together, these three thematic strands in advertising lead Barthes to reaffirm the signifying power of food, though it is necessary to turn to his essays on food and drink in the book *Mythologies* (1973: 58) to gain some detailed illustration of his views. In 'Wine and Milk', Barthes argues that wine is a totem drink together with the milk of the Dutch cow and the tea drunk by the British Royal Family (Barthes's specificity appears to be a stylistic matter, and it is the national associations of these drinks to which he is alluding). Wine, milk and tea can support various mythologies in those cultural contexts where they have particular salience. Within these cultural contexts (and when they are transplanted to different ones), mythologies also offer a great potential for ambiguity and contradiction. Thus, in France, wine is considered an effective thirst-quencher, yet elsewhere it can be perceived as having the potential to dehydrate and make people thirstier. In 'Steak and Chips', Barthes argues that steak is the heart of the meat, meat in its purest state. Whoever eats meat absorbs its bull-like qualities, including strength. Steak is also patriotic and nostalgic, values also imputed to chips, with which steak is routinely associated in culinary terms.

Prized as the apex of all that is good in cuisine, steak is also attributed the virtue of elegance, 'for among the apparent complexity of exotic cooking, it is a food which unites, one feels, succulence and simplicity' (1973: 63). The theme of exotic cuisine is taken up in the essay 'Ornamental Cookery' which focuses on the French magazine for women, *Elle*, read at the time of his writing, according to Barthes, by working-class women. In its treatment of cookery, *Elle* characteristically presented a colour photograph of a prepared dish, an image that emphasised the food's coatings and general presentation rather than the food itself. For Barthes, this emphasis on appearance and garnishings represents a form of creativity and inventiveness which cannot be extended to the food itself. The appearance of the food, its garnishes and dressings are a diversionary 'sleight of hand' designed to draw attention away from the main problem likely to be encountered by the magazine's readership – namely the inability to afford the foods offered up by the magazine. Barthes gives the example of a partridge decorated with cherries. For most people, Barthes argues, the problem is not in affording the cherry garnish but the partridge itself.

Barthes's interest in food, like that of many other social scientists since, is an essentially transitory phase in his output. If the works referred to above represent his most well-known or indulgent treatment of the subject, then it is in his *Elements of Semiology* (1967) that perhaps the most explicit statement of his views on signifying systems is to be found. Barthes's analytic model is based on Saussure's theory of linguistics and in particular the distinction between language (langue) and speech (parole). Language is the set of conventions essential to communication and is distinct from the signs and symbols which it comprises. Speech (parole) is the individual expression of use of language and entails the application of language rules, and the combination of the signs and symbols that make up language for the purpose of individual expression. Speech is thus the individual act of selection and articulation of language. According to Barthes, the alimentary language comprises rules of exclusion (e.g. food taboos); signifying oppositions of elements in the culinary language (e.g. between savoury and sweet); rules of association which work at both the level of the dish and the level of the menu; and rituals of food use. Alimentary speech comprises all the personal, group and national variations of food selection, preparation and association. For Barthes, the menu is the archetypal expression of the relationship between language and speech. Any menu is constructed with reference to the structure of alimentary language, but the structure is filled differently according to the prevailing modes of alimentary speech. What Barthes appears to be arguing (and it is by no means clear) is that alimentary language determines what foods are 'available' for consumption (given prevailing mores and taboos in respect of what is regarded as edible, what foods may be legitimately associated together, and how these foods are to be prepared), and a menu (in the broadest sense, for it does seem that Barthes's use of the term is intended to embrace as much a 'national' menu as any menu that might be presented in a restaurant, or in the home as part of the cycle of domestic consumption) is any given expression of this language. The processes that mediate the relationship between language and speech include those identified by Barthes in his essay 'Towards a psychosociology of contemporary food consumption', but it would be unwise to argue such a position categorically, as Barthes's work on food is unsystematically expressed and lacks clarity. Like much of his writing, Barthes's foray into the sociological analysis of food and eating is tantalising and incomplete, but his influence cannot be ignored, although it has been somewhat marginalised in recent commentaries on the area.

### *Pierre Bourdieu*

Bourdieu's main claim to be included among those theorists who have influenced the sociological analysis of food and eating is his book *Distinction: A Social Critique of the Judgement of Taste* (1984). In this work, Bourdieu examines how 'taste' is formed in respect of a variety of cultural forms, including art, music, clothes and food. Generally regarded as a structuralist Marxist, Bourdieu is adamant that taste is socially shaped and that social class is the main differentiator of taste. Moreover, the hierarchy of taste is itself a reflection of the class hierarchy, and concepts such as 'good taste' and 'bad taste' are largely determined by those in the upper reaches of the social hierarchy who, by virtue of their class position and socio-economic advantage, possess 'cultural capital' which they can employ to impress their cultural world-view on society as a whole.

In the case of food and eating, Bourdieu draws on statistical information on French consumption patterns and notes that as income rises, the proportion of income spent on food diminishes and, within the food budget, the proportion spent on heavy, fattening and cheap foods declines while that spent on leaner, lighter, non-fattening and generally more expensive foods increases. Bourdieu argues that consumption is not a simple function of income and notes that there are cases where, as an indicator, income reveals patterns of consumption that go against what trend data would predict. For example, he notes that 'foremen remain attached to "popular" taste although they earn more than clerical and commercial employees, whose taste differs radically from that of manual workers and is closer to that of teachers' (1984: 177). Bourdieu's response to this seeming paradox is to construct an opposition between tastes of luxury (or freedom) and tastes of necessity (a binary opposition reminiscent of the work of Lévi-Strauss). The former are the tastes of the bourgeois, those who have freedom from necessity by virtue of their economic position. The latter is an expression of the necessities of which the working classes are a product, 'from the necessity of reproducing labour power at the lowest cost which is forced on the proletariat as its very definition' (ibid.). When 'tastes of necessity' are maintained where higher incomes would suggest a greater 'freedom', this may reflect to some degree a continuing commitment to the taste to which the working class are condemned, and a form of cultural resistance. In the latter case, tastes of necessity are reconstituted as tastes of freedom, where freedom is construed as a form of resistance to the greater refinement of taste exhibited by higher social classes: the proletariat deliberately adopts a form of 'congenital coarseness' (1984: 178). These attitudes reflect a lifestyle of spontaneous gratification characteristic of classes lower down the social hierarchy, members of which have little to expect from the future, being the exploited classes with limited scope to influence real events. At the same time, this spontaneous gratification is also an expression of solidarity, of the greater importance of community over the individual.

Bourdieu also considers the relationship between class and gender, suggesting that women in lower social classes tend to fulfil a 'traditional role' that is, *inter alia*, geared towards the time-consuming production of dishes for family consumption. Upper-class women, in contrast, spend more time on child care and the transmission of cultural capital, thereby contesting the traditional concept of the domestic division of labour in respect of food, this being reflected in the practice of using lighter foods that need less preparation and cooking time. This examination of the cultural and symbolic aspects of gender-class relationships is extended in Bourdieu's survey of the differences that exist between classes in the context of family and domestic food consumption. The working-class meal is, he argues, characterised by quantity and by the use of 'elastic' or 'abundant' dishes (1984: 194) such as soups, pastas and potatoes. Food is served with implements like ladles and spoons to avoid too much measuring or counting of foodstuffs and food consumption. Food provision is also marked by gender differentiation. A man's plate is filled twice and the performance of this act for a boy marks his transition from child to man. It is correspondingly met by a reduction of food intake on the part of women, who share single portions or make do with leftovers from previous meals. As Bourdieu puts it, 'It is part of men's status to eat and to eat well (and also to drink well); it is particularly insisted that they should eat, on the grounds that "it won't keep", and there is something suspect about a refusal' (1984: 195). All food for a meal may also be placed on the table at the same time rather than following a strict sequencing of courses, and the same plates can be used throughout the meal. While such behaviour would be interpreted in bourgeois circles as slovenly, it is in fact highly functional, ensuring what Bourdieu terms 'economy of effort'. Men do not participate in housework or the preparation and service of meals because, he argues, women would not allow it as 'it would be a dishonour to see men step outside their rôle' (ibid.). Much food is placed on the table to save constant to-ing and fro-ing. All such actions are possible only in a context of domestic relaxation, among the family, where unnecessary ceremony would be seen as inappropriate.

In bourgeois homes, meals are taken according to what is perceived as 'due form'. This form is a matter of rhythm and embraces a number of rules: waiting until the last person served has started to eat; taking modest portions of food; and following a set sequence of courses (1984: 196). Restraint, decorum and propriety are the key behavioural attitudes here, and any division between the interior world of the home and family, and the external world, is rejected. The meal reflects the bourgeois value of deferred gratification, and acts of food consumption are highly disciplined. Such behaviour is a form of aesthetic: 'correct', 'polite' eating has two principal aesthetic dimensions. The first is the cooking, preparation and, in particular, *presentation* of food. The sequencing of courses, the balance of the meal in terms of content and appearance, and the emphasis on quality rather than quantity, shows effort on the part of the provider, effort directed towards realisation of eating as part of the 'art of living' (ibid.). That such behaviour forms part of the bourgeois code reflects the distance of the bourgeois from eating for necessity. In Bourdieu's terms, it denies the primary function of food consumption, which is nutritional, instead elevating the meal to a social and aesthetic occasion. The second aesthetic dimension to the bourgeois meal is behavioural: the rituals of behaviour in response to the preparation and service of a meal in terms of the characteristics of 'due form' are themselves aesthetic responses that demonstrate proper appreciation of the talents of the cook, whether she (and in Bourdieu's mind it is definitely a she) is the hostess or mistress of the house.

Bourdieu's analysis in the context of French culture is of course ethnocentric but nevertheless revealing. By placing social stratification – and, in particular, class – at the centre of his analysis, Bourdieu is able, through the analysis of statistical trend data, to examine both the material and cultural dimensions to food and eating. When talking of the proletariat's 'congenital coarseness', Bourdieu, as noted earlier, invokes spontaneous gratification to explain working-class conviviality and commitment to the here and now. Interestingly, from the point of view of the structuralist/materialist distinction discussed earlier, Bourdieu remarks:

> It becomes clearer why the practical materialism which is particularly manifested in the relation to food is one of the most fundamental components of the popular ethos and even the popular ethic. The being-in-the-present which is affirmed in the readiness to take advantage of the good times and take time as it comes is, in itself, an affirmation of solidarity with others . . . (Bourdieu, 1984: 183)

Later in his discussion of food, Bourdieu makes further reference to the dialectic between materialism and aestheticism, between the working class, who treat food 'as it is' and approach food in a less hypocritical or at least less ritualistic way than the bourgeoisie, and the latter, who imbue food with all kinds of values other than those relevant to basic nutrition (Bourdieu, 1984: 197–200).

It is at this point that the weaknesses in Bourdieu's position begin to unravel. Valuable though Bourdieu's analysis is, it is tainted by vulgar Marxist sentiment on several issues, and not least in his tendency to valorise the working class, to lend them an idealised and spurious 'nobility' that sees them exploited and put upon, but despite this retaining an honesty and closeness to nature and the natural. This is reflected in the asymmetrical nature of Bourdieu's analysis of working- and middle-class meals. The complex nature of Bourdieu's language makes it difficult to track, but there can be no doubt that, for him, it is largely the bourgeoisie that imbue food with symbolic meanings, it is only in the bourgeoisie that 'tastes for freedom' lead to sophisticated codes of behaviour and ritual that circumscribe behaviour. Similar 'tastes of freedom' among the proletariat are confined to an almost grotesque inversion of the bourgeois code, emphasising 'congenital coarseness', slovenliness and slobbery, behaviour which Bourdieu appears to regard as verging on the heroic. Of course, such action *may* be an expression, as Bourdieu implies, of the collective heroism of the proletariat, but this is not the point. The issue is that much less weight is attached to the cultural and symbolic significance of proletarian dining and proletarian meals. It is as if the abstract (but, for Bourdieu, real) concept of cultural capital is a prerequisite for the weaving of sophisticated myths, meanings and rituals around acts of consumption. Apart from being vaguely patronising, both for reasons of logic and in the light of evidence that will be considered later in this book, such an argument cannot be accepted. As Douglas, in her review of *Distinction*, puts it:

> Unfortunately too, it is difficult to anchor the interpretation to the tables that are given. For example, take the hearty working-class family who are supposed in the text to sweep away petty distinctions of table service, to be lavishly hospitable and careless of form with their close friends and family. They are said not to submit to eating to form . . . But when we look at the detailed answers we see that it is the working classes who prefer to offer their guests 'a real menu' rather than a buffet. What is that if not eating within forms? It is the working classes who say they like to end a festive meal with singing and

to fill the evening with parlour games – distinctly formal to this reviewer's middle-class eye. (Douglas, 1982c: 131)

## Marvin Harris

Together with Stephen Mennell, Marvin Harris is, perhaps, the most virulent anti-structuralist writer on food. His opposition to the arguments of writers like Lévi-Strauss and Mary Douglas is almost evangelical (see especially Harris, 1986; 1987). Harris describes these writers as cultural idealists and notes:

> In general, cultural idealists explain variations in food preferences and aversions as a consequence of 'culture' (by which they mean the learned emic and mental components of social life). This strategy has resulted in three kinds of explanatory propositions: (1) food customs are said to be the consequence of idiographic-historical continuities that regress to an unknown beginning; (2) they are the consequence of arbitrary 'taste', chance, or whim; (3) they are the functional symbolic or behavioural correlates or expressions of given systems of values and beliefs. To the extent that none of these varieties of propositions invoke selection principles that can account for specific observed variations in food customs (as well as uniformities) or for the occurrence of the constraining values and beliefs, they constitute a weak form of scientific statement or none at all. (Harris, 1987: 57)

In more specific terms, Harris latches on to Lévi-Strauss's assertion that 'food is a kind of language whose attributes are "good to think" because they unconsciously express fundamental themes in the human psyche' (1987: 59). Harris is quick to note, as have other authors, that no empirical evidence has been forthcoming in support of the concept of the culinary triangle (see for example Goody, 1982: 215–20). A more significant criticism by Harris of Lévi-Strauss concerns the latter's lack of particularism. Harris suggests that even if the culinary triangle were an adequate representation of universal structure in food, it still would not explain variations between societies in the selection of some foodstuffs rather than others, as well as predilections for modes of food preparation.

Lévi-Strauss's universalism is, of course, at the heart of Mary Douglas's rejection of his work and one of the motivating factors in her own micro-sociological analysis of foodways. Harris, however, remains unconvinced by Douglas's work. He depicts her studies of meals as devoid of any consideration of how symbolic values and meanings expressed in food choice and food use relate to economic, nutritional and dietary factors. For Harris, 'the issue is the extent to which the selection of foods to convey meaning is an autonomous process that can be understood apart from the processes that are responsible for selecting foods for nourishment; or, in more extreme forms of idealism, whether the selection of foods to convey meaning actually dominates the selection of foods for nourishment' (Harris, 1987: 60). Harris's intellectual enmity towards Douglas seems to be reciprocated (or, more accurately, anticipated) by Douglas (1984), who writes, somewhat tersely:

> Marvin Harris' work . . . has potentially powerful insights for interpreting long-term changes. But the method is inevitably weak for observing short-term relations between social factors and perceived needs. Furthermore, it assumes rational economic choice for explaining cultural adaptation, but . . . this is precisely the assumption that is challenged in the current thinking about food tastes. The modern consumer has lost credibility as a rational agent in the eyes of food theorists. So this distinctly anthropological approach lacks fine-tuned relevance to the way that the great food problems are posed. (Douglas, 1984: 8).

Harris characterises his own approach to the sociological study of food and eating as one of 'cultural materialism'. Two assumptions are embodied in this approach. The first is that biological, psychological, environmental, technological, political and economic factors *all* influence the foods that can be consumed in a given context. The second is that whatever symbolic or social meanings are attached to food, all humans must satisfy basic nutritional needs, and psychological and chemical limits of 'taste and toxic tolerances' must be observed (Harris, 1987: 58). Harris accepts that foods convey aesthetic and symbolic meanings and messages and that sometimes these meanings and messages are arbitrary in nature (Harris, 1986: 15; 1987: 61). His main objection to the idealist approach lies in a somewhat sophisticated 'chicken and egg' problem, in that he believes that for the most part, whether foods are 'good or bad to think' depends on whether they are good or bad to eat. He argues that 'Food must nourish the collective stomach before it can feed the collective mind' (1986: 15). This leads him to assert that food preferences – 'good-to-eat' foods – are those which offer a more favourable balance of practical benefits over costs than those that are avoided – 'bad-to-eat' foods. These costs and benefits can be assessed over a range of criteria, for example, whether or not foods are, in terms of economics and effort, worth producing and preparing; whether or not some foods have cheaper and more nutritious substitutes; and whether or not the cultivation of some foods may be damaging to a particular environment.

Douglas's view of some of Harris's earlier work has already been noted, but other criticisms have been advanced. Murcott (1988: 19–20) makes three important observations. First, she suggests that Harris's theoretical approach is ill-suited to explaining the learned preferences for elaborate eating evident among the European aristocracy in the eighteenth century. This argument can be extended to cover the subsequent developments of 'refined' eating right up to the present day (see Wood, 1991). Second, Murcott identifies a tension in Harris's work between his insistence on food selection, production and preparation as primarily a matter of the assessment of costs and benefits, and his view that such considerations can easily incorporate, in addition, ecological and nutritional considerations. Third, like Douglas, Murcott questions Harris's depiction of food consumers as intrinsically rational in the choices they make, suggesting that the weight of interdisciplinary evidence indicates a contrary view.

Murcott's critique of Harris is characteristically neutral. A more pungent assessment is provided by Fiddes in his outstanding study *Meat: A Natural Symbol* (1991). Fiddes rejects Harris's view that humans are in some way genetically programmed to prefer animal foods, arguing that scientific evidence does not support this view. For Fiddes (1991: 14), 'instinct' is a more appropriate topic, than tool, for analysis, and he accordingly locates the study of food selection and preferences in the social realm. He is also particularly scathing of Harris's suggestion that preference for meat in so many societies is a product of utility and scarcity, of meat's inherent nutritional value and the economic investment and hardship required to produce it. Harris's economics does indeed appear somewhat simplistic, and Fiddes plays on this, pointing to the great variations across societies in the value placed on meat, as well as the preference of many individuals and some societies for a vegetarian diet.

While it may appear that criticisms of Harris's position have been fairly harsh, it is the case, as Murcott notes, that his views are typical of an established North American approach to the social anthropology of food and nutrition. There would, therefore, be some expectation of intellectual hostility from those in rival theoretical camps. Harris's arguments are polemical, ironically, 'good to think', a useful exercise in forceful didacticism that at the very least challenges those not persuaded by the materialistic case to argue alternative positions with clarity and circumspection.

### *Jack Goody*

Like Bourdieu, the social anthropologist Jack Goody's reputation as a theoretical commentator on the social aspects of food and eating rests mainly on the strength of one book, *Cooking, Cuisine and Class* (1982). He, like Harris, recognises the strength of structuralism while being critical of it. As Murcott (1988: 25) implies, however, Goody is unlike Harris in that he is concerned to recognise structuralist perspectives as complementary to other forms of analysis:

> Despite the framework of opposition given to or assumed by the various approaches I have discussed in the context of the sociology of cooking, it is clear that they are not so much alternatives as complementary, at least in some of their aspects . . . much of the disagreement lies not at the level of theoretical practice but of theoretical assertion. (Goody, 1982: 33)

Goody sees structuralism as failing to appreciate the material aspects of dietary habits and consumption: structuralism is seen as removed from some 'real world' of hard choices that all stem from the physiological requirement to eat to live. This reading is supported by Goody's assertion that in structuralist terminology, phrases like 'deciphering a code' suggest 'a defined and objectively determined locus and content of "meaning"' (1982: 32).

This is an interesting observation in that a central theme in structuralist writing is that while it is possible to discern patterns of meaning from the relationships among signs and symbols (social phenomena), these patterns can and do change, and the realm of objective meaning is largely a positivistic fiction. What in fact is happening here is that Goody is making a rather subtle case against structural approaches. He notes how writers in the tradition of 'Parisian structuralism' 'decode' cultural phenomena in different ways, utilising different terms and making different assumptions. This leads Goody to suggest that 'the existence of any such objectively determinable relations seems somewhat doubtful' (1982: 32). This enjoyably slick form of reasoning is, sadly, faulty, if only because many structuralists would probably agree with Goody on this last point. What Goody does is impute a spurious quality to structuralists' claims (that it seeks some form of objective and absolute reality and meaning) and then use evidence of the plurality of structuralist approaches to demonstrate that such meaning is unattainable. Like most materialist/developmental writers who claim to recognise the importance of structuralist contributions to the study of food and eating, Goody neatly sidesteps any in-depth analysis of such contributions, instead prosecuting his own theoretical agenda. For Goody, structural approaches play down the role of history in understanding how food behaviours evolve and develop. Structuralists' ignorance of the role of history and their preference for the 'here and now' is regarded as a critical flaw in their reasoning. However, Goody's own view of the role of history in the development of food habits is not easy to pin down since, as Murcott (1988: 29) notes, his analysis has a rather static feel to it.

One reason for this is that Goody's other major interest – 'class' – tends to dominate his work, and historical analysis in *Cooking, Cuisine and Class* is undertaken in a highly uneven manner, a fact reflected in the breadth of evidence that Goody utilises – from a study of Ghanaian tribes to Ancient Egypt, India and China, and the industrialised food of the West. Goody's central theme is simple enough. He is concerned to discover why, in some societies, a high (élite) and low (peasant) cuisine emerges, where in other societies it does not. Social and political complexity cannot be the cause as, Goody asserts, many African societies exhibit such complexity without ever having developed a differentiated cuisine. The degree of such complexity may be important, however, as, within certain African societies, the various levels of differentiation are relatively fluid, with close relationships between the different strata. Also of importance is the level of literacy in a society. Prior to the development of mass literacy, Goody argues, societies tend to be stratified in this one dimension according to who has access to the written word. This can lead to differentiation in other cultural spheres, as the literate enjoy more opportunities and life chances, and emphasise their distinctiveness in matters of taste and lifestyle, including cuisine. A final set of reasons which Goody identifies as germane to the development of high/low cuisines in certain societies is the sexual division of labour. Goody's contribution here is highly generalised but nevertheless interesting. He suggests that the sexual division of labour in African and Eurasian societies is based on different, complex, kinship relationships which reflect different relationships between the symbolic and material value of foods. Thus, in African societies, cooking is largely the domain of women throughout the hierarchy of social strata, and the types of food served reflect the basic domestic cuisine of these societies. In Eurasian societies, cooking for the élite is normally in the hands of servants and male cooks and chefs, with women largely confined to cooking in the home. The connection between these developments and the development of high and low cuisines is not altogether clear in Goody's work, partly because the very complexity and interplay of influences deny the possibility of asserting causality in the differentiation of cuisine. Capitalist industrialisation may, in conventional sociological terms, account for the gendered division of labour, but many of the societies Goody has in mind, where men cook in the public sphere and women in the domestic, exhibit gendered labour in the absence of industrial capitalism. The sweep of Goody's work means that he does not follow through many of his arguments in a systematic fashion, and there is limited mileage in attempting to second-guess his meaning. In contrast to the emphatic style of writers like Douglas and Harris, Goody's analysis permits neither of direct answers nor of the possibility of 'filling in the gaps' by means of supposition as to his intent.

### Stephen Mennell via Norbert Elias

Stephen Mennell has made a number of contributions to sociological and social historical analysis of food and eating, but the most important is undoubtedly his magisterial *All Manners of Food: Eating and Taste in England and France from the Middle Ages to the Present* (1985). In this book, Mennell rejects structuralist analyses of cuisine and advocates an alternative theoretical position which he characterises as developmental. It was noted earlier how this term is insisted upon by Mennell in contrast to the label 'materialist' (Mennell, Murcott and van Otterloo, 1992). Mennell's main intellectual inspiration in both theory and method is the work of Norbert Elias, whose contribution to Mennell's thought, as well as to the sociology of food and eating more generally, is often underrated. Elias's contribution will be considered here prior to a more detailed assessment of Mennell's work.

A refugee from the Germany of Hitler, Elias settled in England for a time. His most important work, *The Civilizing Process*, was first published in German in 1939 but did not become available in English translation (in two volumes) until 1978 and 1982. The key concept in Elias's work is the figuration which is 'a structure of mutually oriented and dependent people' (1978: 261). The central idea here is that of interdependence, as can be seen in the four principal features of the figurational approach (Rojek, 1985: 160–1). These are as follows. First, the major focus of analysis is the figuration, which is conceptualised as an irreducible social unit. Figurations are themselves viewed as comprising multiple networks of interdependence which both constrain and enable the activities of individuals and groups. The irreducibility of figurations leads, secondly, to the view that they are produced and reproduced by individuals over time but that the component parts of a figuration alone cannot explain a figuration's integration and dynamics. As Elias puts it:

The network of interdependencies among human
beings is what binds them together . . . Since people
are more or less dependent on each other first by
nature and then through social learning . . . they
exist, one might venture to say, only as pluralities,
only in figurations. That is why, as was stated earlier,
it is not particularly fruitful to conceive of men in the
image of the individual man. It is more appropriate
to envisage an image of numerous interdependent
people forming figurations (i.e., groups or societies
of different kinds) with each other. (1978: 261)

Elias (1978: 262) goes on to remark that figurations are relatively
independent of the specific individuals who comprise them
but not of individuals *per se*. This leads, thirdly, to the observation that the development of figurations may be influenced by
the actions of individuals engaged in planned intervention, but
such development, in terms of the interdependencies that bind
people together at each point in the growth of a figuration, are
generally not planned or willed by the individuals who comprise it. Here, Elias appears to be suggesting that to some
extent, any figuration has a life of its own, over and above individual's individual motivations. He writes that 'a change in a
figuration is explained partly by the endogenous dynamic of
the figuration itself' (1978: 262), a clear reaffirmation of the
point that the figuration, with all its complexities, is a basic
social unit that cannot be reduced further for analytic purposes.

The fourth and final aspect of the figurational approach concerns the manner in which the first three characteristics are to
be articulated in research. For Elias, the study of social relations
is necessarily a study of interaction and interdependencies
among people. More important, however, is the fact that these
interdependencies should be studied processually. As Elias
puts it, 'structure theories . . . embody the spatial dimensions.
They have . . . the character of three-dimensional models.
Process theories have the character of four-dimensional models
. . . they do not abstract from either the spatial or the time
dimension (Elias, 1974: 40, quoted in Rojek, 1985: 160–1). Elias's
own major illustration of the processual approach to the study
of society is his *The Civilizing Process*. The term 'civilising

process' refers to a specific set of changes which have supposedly taken place in human personality structure since the Middle Ages. These changes have involved trends towards much greater levels of self-discipline and self-control, and rising standards of shame and embarrassment in interpersonal interaction. Elias (1978) illustrates these trends in fine historical detail, drawing on a wide range of documents and, in particular, various commentaries on 'appropriate' social conduct, or 'savoir-vivre', many of the earlier examples of which were directed towards guiding people's behaviour 'at court' (Elias argues that the new standards of behaviour established from the Middle Ages on were largely the product of the secular upper class but, by a process of diffusion, many such standards filtered down the social order, though the process was slow and uneven – given the 'ongoing' nature of the civilising process, this diffusion is presumably a studied feature of behavioural trends originating in the upper reaches of the social hierarchy).

Examples of the trend towards more civilised behaviour abound (the first volume of *The Civilizing Process* is in fact entitled *The History of Manners*: Elias, 1978). The documentation which Elias draws upon includes guidelines on spitting, defecating, urinating, and behaviour in the bedroom. Charted over time, these historical documents show an exhortation to greater self-restraint and decorum. For the present purpose, it is Elias's study of behaviour at table which is most germane. Greater refinement, he argues, can be seen to develop in a number of ways. Since the basic technology of eating was established – the use of implements, knives, forks and spoons – among the French upper classes prior to the Revolution, little has changed in terms of the *essential* form of these implements, though they have been substantially differentiated within their own type. Thus there are many different types of fork, knife and spoon for use in eating different types of food, the presentation of which at meals has itself become more differentiated. What applies to cutlery also applies to plates. Since medieval times there has been a move away from eating from a common bowl at meals to more individualised, 'dainty' or civilised habits. Plates and cutlery have become the norm, but, over time, differentiation has led to a situation whereby these are changed after each course, and different types of cutlery and crockery relevant to the consumption of particular types of food (soup, corn-on-the-cob, for example) or categories of food (starter, main course, dessert) have become the norm. Related to this analysis is the observation that with the move away from the common bowl comes the development of more precise portioning, itself partly a function of the development of discrete 'courses' which introduce a sequence of relatively constrained quantities of food into meals, more or less clearly defining the beginning and end of meals and therefore defining the quantity of food available.

Elias's commentary on the development of mealtime etiquette and technology in the context of the civilising process is useful in combining a symbolic and historical analysis of change. However, a key problem with the figurational approach is that it is a single-explanation theory – everything can be reduced in explanatory terms to the effects of the civilising process. Even if the trend towards civility and refinement is an enduring one, figurationalism does little to account for the varying symbolic significance attached to different types of meals, or foodstuffs, or different types of eating implements. The meanings of such variations are submerged in a great, ongoing, historical process that seeks to explain cultural change at a fairly high level of generalisation. The civilising process is a *deus ex machina* for the explanation of cultural change. In this way, attention is directed away from the detail of figurational change itself, away from an understanding of those forces and influences that themselves constitute the civilising process.

There are other objections to the figurational approach, and these can best be illustrated by returning to the work of Mennell (1985). He emphatically rejects structuralist approaches to the study of food and eating, claiming that structuralism tends towards the static and is of little use in explaining how tastes change and develop over time. He writes that 'structuralist and cultural "explanations" of food preferences really add little to the old argument that "people like what they are used to" – they offer mainly a classificatory scheme, not an explanation' (1985: 13). Mennell is also extremely dismissive of individual structuralist writers. For example, he dispatches Barthes, saying 'Barthes was writing specifically about the *contemporary* food system and, characteristically as a structuralist, expected to be able to derive his "grammar" without reference to history. The past was simply a place where potent meanings could be quarried, for example by advertisers' (1985: 11–12). Now, all this could easily be accepted as part of the routine of academic cut-and-thrust if it were not for the fact that Mennell's dismissal of structuralism and structuralists is very offhand.

To demonstrate this, it is necessary to stay close to Mennell's text. The crucial passage in his destruction of structuralism is the remark that 'The structuralist preoccupation with codes and deep structures is a striking example of this [process reduction]: not only are the codes apparently depicted as static and unchanging but so, as often as not, are the patterns of social relations which they are supposed to "express"' (1985: 14). In this passage, Mennell is pursuing the claim that structuralist theories tend towards a state of 'process reduction' – the search for stasis and structure, a search doomed in Mennell's view because society is always in a state of flux, always changing. Few people would disagree with this. It is certainly true that sociologists, like many other academics, are predominantly concerned with the here and now. The argument presented by writers like Goody, Elias and Mennell, that sociologists largely ignore history, is therefore a true one. It is not in itself a very persuasive argument, however, and is a little like accusing heart surgeons of being indifferent to dentistry. As directed towards structuralists in particular, Mennell does, however, have a small point. For example, Culler writes that structural explanation 'does not seek historical antecedents or causes but discusses the structure and significance of particular objects or actions by relating them to the system within which they function' (1983: 79). Other structuralist writers hold to this view, but it is doubtful that Mennell's criticisms can be applied to all structuralists. Certainly, Mennell does not establish this beyond reasonable doubt and his earlier noted criticism of Barthes does not stand close scrutiny. Barthes makes no pretence of his primary concern with the contemporary meanings imputed to food and eating, but to dismiss his work because it fails to address adequately the role of historical forces and influences on contemporary eating is like dismissing the work of any academic social scientist whose research into contemporary social phenomena did not take account of the 'role of history'.

Mennell's polemical style is one thing. What makes his

critique of structuralism harder to swallow are the inconsistencies evident in his alternative approach. Crudely speaking, figurationalism is about putting history back into sociology. For Mennell, however, history is not enough. He rejects a view of history as being simply a question of identifying 'a chronological catalogue of ill-assorted "factors" and episodes which from time to time have had some effect on this aspect or that aspect of what people liked and disliked to eat' (1985: 15). While historical research is certainly more than just a matter of chronology, this looks suspiciously like a plea for some kind of sanitised history. This is, in fact, what it turns out to be. Mennell continues: 'To go beyond that, it is necessary to look carefully at the jumbled historical record to see if it is possible to discern not constants beneath the flux, but an order of a different kind, a sequential order constituting *structured processes of change*' (1985: 15).

Any sensible reading of this passage can yield only one conclusion, namely that sociologists should not, emphatically not, search for 'constants beneath the flux', for structures persistent over time: they are to be largely ignored even where they might exist. Instead, it is the search for another kind of structure that it is to take priority – 'structured processes of change'. The problem is that in the case of both Elias and Mennell, it is not altogether clear what these, in a general conceptual sense, might be. In *All Manners of Food*, this lack of clarity is exacerbated by the absence of any coherent attempt by Mennell to develop these themes throughout the main body of the text. As Murcott puts it, 'He does not always tie up a chapter in the light of the question he posed at its beginning and is inclined to introduce key bits of his argument in the middle of a paragraph . . .' (1988: 33). While in no manner denigrating the immense scholarship which *All Manners of Food* represents – it is, in respect of range and detail, simply magnificent – Mennell simply fails to persuade when it comes to hitching his empirical survey of changes in English and French eating habits since the Middle Ages to his figurationalist theoretical perspective.

Only in the final chapter of *All Manners of Food* does some indication of what is meant by 'structured processes of change' appear. Here, Mennell argues in the case of his own historical survey that there is evidence over time of 'diminishing contrasts' and 'increasing varieties' between certain food-related habits, attitudes and beliefs. Contrasts between seasonal eating patterns on the one hand, and everyday eating on the other, have also diminished, largely as a result of advances in technology and transportation that allow more foods and more varieties of food to be available more of the time. Similarly, the contrasts have diminished between élite professional cookery and everyday cooking: peasant dishes have been absorbed into haute cuisine; cookery guides and cookery books have 'spread appreciation of good cookery to *wider* audiences than before' (Mennell, 1985: 326); and the growth of the hotel and restaurant industry since the nineteenth century has encouraged culinary democracy because such establishments were, and have continued to be, more public, less exclusive places, to the extent that while eating out is still influenced by class, 'The social stratification of eating-places has become still more blurred in the late twentieth century' (1985: 326).

The increasing varieties to which Mennell refers can be detected over time in the proliferation of dishes; the differentiation of public restaurants and private households; the differentiation of many kinds of restaurant; and the creation of a competitive market for both domestic and non-domestic foodstuffs. More significantly, all these processes represent a growth in culinary pluralism and a decline in the prestige hierarchy of food which places French haute cuisine at its apex. The growth of culinary pluralism is evidence of parallel processes in other arts, namely the loss of a single dominant style, and the mixing of styles together as a defining feature of culinary practice, for example on menus. In Britain, culinary pluralism has been encouraged by a market-oriented catering industry and the acceptance of outside influences such as oriental and Asian cuisines and American food.

All these assertions are signalled, though developed with varying coherence, in the central body of Mennell's book, and some do not always appear sustainable. The idea that the contrasts have diminished between élite professional cookery and everyday cookery is a bizarre one and, in a different context, has been systematically refuted elsewhere (Wood, 1991). Here, Mennell confuses process with product. It may be true that elements of haute cuisine are, as products, readily reproducible in the home in the form of frozen ingredients, ready meals or whatever. It may be that elements of what are accepted as part of the repertoire of haute cuisine can be reproduced for domestic consumption. The point about élite professional cookery, however, is that the cookery process itself is only a part of the total product, which also embraces style, service and conspicuous public consumption that cannot be reproduced entirely in the home and is a necessarily 'public' phenomenon. In supporting his argument, Mennell notes the absorption of peasant cuisine into haute cuisine. It does not require any great intellectual skill to identify the objection that the acceptance of non-élite foodstuffs into an élite repertoire does not necessarily diminish the contrast between 'peasant' and élite food. Nor for that matter does the proliferation of various media spreading an 'appreciation' of 'good' cookery to wider audiences necessarily give rise to such an effect. Who, in any case, is to determine what 'good' cookery is? Further, the assertion that hotels and restaurants encourage culinary democracy borders on the factually unsustainable, as does the idea that the social stratification of eating places has become increasingly blurred. Analyses of this highly fragmented industry by sociologists and others lead to an opposite conclusion, and this is no minority viewpoint. The stratification of the modern hospitality industry focuses divisions, divisions of class, of gender and of taste (see for example Carmouche, 1980; Saunders, 1981; Riley, 1984; Urry, 1990; Wood, 1992b; 1994).

At a more general level of criticism, if Mennell is arguing that tensions exist between complex social trends and phenomena, and that it is difficult to delineate a neat, uniform model or description of what is actually 'going on', all well and good. However, this offers no more of an explanation of food habits than the structuralism which he so crushingly dismisses. In her review of Mennell's book, Murcott writes of the 'persistent suspicion that Mennell is prey to some sort of "foodie" partisanship' (1986b: 646). This would certainly explain the valorisation of French haute cuisine which is arguably accorded a superior analytic status in *All Manners of Food*. Murcott sees such influences as of minor importance, and in terms of the overall status of Mennell's enormous scholarship she is undoubtedly correct. However, in the context of the critical annihilation of structuralism executed by Mennell, and the strength (or rather weakness) of his alternative case for figurationalism, any such 'foodie partisanship' may be one element in an explanation of why many of Mennell's arguments fail to convince.

## THEORETICAL RESOLUTIONS

In the conclusion to her 1988 review of developments in the field of the sociology of food and eating, Murcott suggested that three trends were apparent. The first was social anthropology's continuing concern with food and eating and the beginnings of such interest in sociology. The second was the potential for food and eating to become of central analytic importance in each discipline. The third, and for Murcott most important, was 'that the strengths of discussions and debates about the merits of different modes of analysis already well under way in each discipline, are explicitly and more systematically being drawn into the specific sociological and social anthropological literature on human food habits, preferences and cuisines' (Murcott, 1988: 34). While this remark may have been appropriate in 1988, with hindsight it appears over-optimistic. The 'different modes of analysis' to which Murcott refers in effect boil down to the structuralist-developmentalist opposition in theoretical contributions to the field, the framework that was broadly followed in the previous section. But what of the reliability of the framework itself?

Despite its considerable value to the analysis of theorising in the sociology of cuisine, the most important reservation about Murcott's framework in both its original and modified form is that close reading of the work of those writers which the framework embraces makes for the unavoidable conclusion that the central dichotomy between structuralists and materialist/developmentalist writers is a false one, in which case it is possible to agree with Murcott (1988) that the sociological study of cuisine is characterised by diversity but difficult to see why it is thus necessary to construct a framework which conflates such differences into a handy structuralist-developmentalist shorthand. The central issue is a simple one. Whether in its original or modified form, Murcott's framework gives an exaggerated sense of homogeneity to the work of both structuralist and materialist-developmentalist writers. Further, the modified framework (Mennell, Murcott and van Otterloo, 1992) evidences a rhetorical quality. Here, the structuralist-developmentalist division has become more concrete and the framework as a whole more broadly presented as state of the analytic art, a point reflected in one reviewer's comment that 'anyone seeking an introductory map of current knowledge and analytic approaches to food practices . . . could do no better than to consult this book as an initial point of reference' (Warde, 1994: 351).

While it is possible to concur with Warde's general sentiments, Murcott's framework cannot be regarded as either wholly accurate or wholly complete. In terms of accuracy, the dichotomous classification of writers into structuralists and materialists/developmentalists is simplistic and creates ambiguities. For example, structuralism is certainly a diverse school of social theory, but writers like Barthes, Lévi-Strauss and Bourdieu – Goody's 'Parisian structuralists' (Goody, 1982: 32) – have more in common with each other than the likes of Mary Douglas. Furthermore, although a structuralist, Bourdieu is heavily influenced by Marxist thought, and this leads him to lend great weight to the material aspects of food consumption. In this respect, he has a good deal more in common with Elias and Mennell than with, say, Douglas and Harris. The position of Bourdieu also highlights another point, namely the tendency of the polarised structuralist-developmentalist model to heighten the impression of two sides in dialogue with one another. This is simply not the case. Barthes stands apart from all the other writers in terms of both time and specialism. Douglas's early work was in part a reaction against, or response to, Lévi-Strauss, and the debate or dialogue between Douglas and Harris is, at the theoretical level, very much one between social anthropologists first and structuralists and materialists second (Douglas's contributions in particular are very much couched in terms of global anthropological concerns). Mennell's earlier noted objection to the term 'materialist' and his preference for 'developmental' and its variants is understandable, as he does not share the explicit interests and orientations of either Harris or Mintz, or indeed of any of the other major critics of structuralism. Here, there is another problem, however, for, as Murcott (1988) notes, there is little that is particularly developmental about the work of Harris, or for that matter Goody. It does nobody any great service to lump together materialists such as Harris and figurationalists such as Elias and Mennell under the single heading of 'developmental' writers because the two positions *are* very different and the single term disguises the rich diversity of individual contributions.

Does any of this matter? The answer is yes. Accuracy in

modelling theoretical debate in any field of study is crucial in informing empirical research. Any theoretical model must also allow for the incorporation of new perspectives or variants on existing ones. This leads to consideration of the completeness of the Murcott framework as represented in its modified form (Mennell, Murcott and van Otterloo, 1992). Here, there are omissions. Given that several of the authors considered within the boundaries of the framework are included by virtue of one dominant literary contribution, it might have been expected that the work of Joanne Finkelstein would figure in the theoretical mélange. Finkelstein's *Dining Out* (1989) is an important contribution to theoretical development and empirical research in an area largely ignored by sociologists of food and eating. For the purposes of the present discussion, it is sufficient to note that Finkelstein seeks to navigate the theoretical minefield between structuralism and developmentalism in order to forge a distinctive perspective of her own that eschews the excesses of each (see Chapter 3). This is also true to a large degree of a single and singular contribution to theorising in the field by Beardsworth and Keil (1990), who point out that many sociological studies of food consumption have been undertaken to illustrate social processes other than the nature of food consumption itself. They consider it unlikely that the sociological study of food will emerge as a key area of interest unless such an approach can be avoided: more well-conducted empirical case studies with good theoretical underpinning would be helpful for expanding the range of the field but would be unlikely to improve the status generally accorded to the sociology and social anthropology of food and eating within their respective disciplines. The strength of Beardsworth and Keil's contribution lies in the assertion of the primacy of acts of food consumption. They write:

> The problem is that in most sociological studies of dietary practices, food consumption patterns are all too often seen mainly as dependent variables, to be explained with reference to the conventional sociological repertoire of forces, symbols, classes, figurations, categories, gender relations and so on. Yet . . . food consumption is an absolutely fundamental

aspect of human activity. It imposes imperatives
which can, of course, be satisfied in immensely
diverse ways, giving rise to sometimes bewildering
variability. (Beardsworth and Keil, 1990: 148)

Eager to avoid throwing the baby out with the bathwater,
Beardsworth and Keil suggest that while biologically deterministic explanations of food consumption are undesirable, it is
clearly necessary to recognise that biological imperatives 'in
their culturally mediated manifestations, may need to be
accorded *some* causal and formative significance if effective
sociological theories are to be developed in this area' (1990:
149). In this sense, they sail very close to the materialist wind
but, in so doing, avoid falling into the trap of particularism or,
more accurately, theoretical specificity. They advocate a sociology of food and eating that integrates analysis of human food
consumption into a framework which recognises the power of
human culture within a network of associated species of plants
and animals (in other words, a fusion of the natural, materialist,
dimensions to food consumption with the symbolic, structuralist-
aesthetic, dimensions). The value of this proposition lies in the
extent to which food systems are viewed as routinely dynamic.
The need to eat does not simply determine food preferences;
nor are the symbolic qualities imputed to food necessarily
arbitrary. Rather, the biological imperative, the need to eat,
influences the nature and quality of food symbolism which in
turn influences the nature and form of the biological imperative. In other words, there is a 'feedback' process at work, and
this emphasises the interdependency of the material and the
symbolic.

Integration is also the concern of Fischler (1988a) whom, as
previously noted, Mennell, Murcott and van Otterloo (1992)
claim for their own as a structuralist whose work has moved,
theoretically speaking, towards a developmentalist standpoint.
If Finkelstein and Beardsworth and Keil are ignored in Mennell,
Murcott and van Otterloo's framework for the analysis of theory
in the sociology of food and eating, then Fischler's position is
somewhat glossed. In fact, Fischler (1988b) anticipates much of
Beardsworth and Keil's analysis. Focusing in particular on the
materialist position of writers like Harris, and the structuralist
claims of Lévi-Strauss and Douglas, he notes with some asperity

that 'the issue between materialism and structuralism really is which determinism is pre-eminent: ecological or social' (1988b: 201–2). This is an interesting slant on the structuralist-developmentalist dichotomy, for Fischler views each as equally deterministic – the determinism of materialism is in insisting on the biological imperative, the need to eat to survive. The determinism of structuralism derives from its insistence that only culture can explain culture. To reconcile these differences, Fischler proposes an integrative approach, integrative 'in the sense that it takes into account biological as well as social dimensions of the phenomena' (1988b: 203). The resulting model differs from that offered by Beardsworth and Keil in their recognition of biological imperatives. Fischler argues that humans face an 'omnivore's paradox' whereby they face freedom of food choice, a freedom which also constrains them because there must be a minimal variety in the diet in order to provide all necessary nutrients. The constraint of variety means that omnivores must innovate in their food habits but also protect themselves against possible toxicity in foods. The paradoxical consequence of this is that omnivores must identify new food resources in case they are needed, but simultaneously guard against possible poisoning. The tension between neophilia and neophobia is one between the need for change and variety, and fear of the unknown with its concomitant resistance to change. Food habits may be seen to assist the resolution of this paradox in that:

> at the core of every cuisine are peculiar flavour combinations, or 'flavour principles', which function as ethnic markers, indicating familiarity. In fact, the whole of cuisine can be seen as serving this function. Through cooking, food acquires both familiarity and variety. A familiar, monotonous staple can be prepared in an almost infinite number of ways, while a novel food's potential menace can be 'tamed', as it were, by preparing it in familiar ways. (Fischler, 1988b: 204)

This model is interesting but flawed. For example, it takes insufficient account of constraints on food supply – 'freedom' is only a meaningful concept in terms of food choice when supplies are secure and a whole host of other socio-economic conditions are satisfied. Also, the reductionist dependency on psycho-physiological concepts such as 'flavour principles' is an appeal to an unquantified and controversial explanatory variable that can be neither adequately refuted nor substantiated.

As presented by many writers, compromise between structuralist and materialist/developmental perspectives presents seemingly irreconcilable difficulties, a tension between the immovable objects of culture and the irresistible force of nature. Yet theoretical resolution, or at least development, should be possible. To achieve this, it is necessary to accept that sociologists have theorised ahead of themselves to the extent that key positions are entrenched when in fact they need not be. A corollary of this view is that the postulated opposition between structuralist and developmental analyses should not be seen as set in stone. Neither of these theoretical approaches, nor any of the varied positions within them, commands sufficient empirical support to warrant the confident assertions that have emanated, and continue to emanate, from each camp. Both material and cultural factors influence food habits. As Beardsworth and Keil (1990) suggest, the interrelationships between biological needs and cultural values are important to any understanding of how such habits come into being and are sustained and developed. The evident common sense which they express when arguing against treating food habits as a dependent variable is refreshing. Furthermore, notwithstanding the main concerns of the sociologist, it may be wise to accept that some food habits, like other expressions of human behaviour and belief, are a product of individual cognitive preferences or even serendipity. There is necessary sociological sense in identifying regularities in human behaviour, but once these start to be ascribed to some determining influence or influences, whether these be biological imperatives, structure, or civilising processes, then there is a danger that attempts at theoretical explication become instances of obscurantist theoretical dogma.

Of course, in every branch of intellectual endeavour, there are those whose analyses tend towards the radical, and such radicalism has its uses. It serves no purpose, however, for radicals of any persuasion to exaggerate the arguments or perceived intent of their opponents. For example, it makes little sense for Mennell (1985) to assert that structuralism tells us little more than 'people like what they are used to'. One might state with equal justification that figurationalism tells us little more than 'things change'. The explanatory power of figurationalist analysis can be no more easily dismissed than structuralist or more avowedly materialist approaches. Concepts like the 'civilising process', 'diminishing contrasts' and 'increasing varieties' have undoubted relevance to the study of the cultural dimensions to food and eating. It is not necessary, however, to accept the wider theoretical apparatus of figurationalism in recognising the value of such concepts. Nor is it necessary to accept at face value any or all of the illustrative exemplars that are advanced in support of the theoretical case for figurationalism. The same is true for any other theoretical approach, including structuralism.

This long review has sacrificed expediency in discussing theoretical development in the sociology of food and eating to detailed excavation of prevailing theoretical frameworks and perspectives in the field. Notwithstanding the very real value of such debates, it is suggested that a more circumspect and flexible approach to theorising in the sociology of food and eating is required, one that emphasises the diversity of individual theoretical contributions to the field. If there must be a framework, something along the lines of that shown in Figure 1.3 might provide a starting point. This model divorces the figurationalist perspective from the materialist. For reasons identified earlier, this can be justified on the grounds that both perspectives are distinctive in orientation. Writers in both traditions have in common an opposition to structuralist analyses, and there are other points of similarity. There are, equally, points of substantial difference that legitimate this more clearly delimited model of theoretical debate in the area. The model offers a distinction between radicals and pragmatists. These terms are not intended to be used pejoratively, but merely as descriptions of the relative positions of different contributors to theoretical development in the field. Hence, in each area, the radical-pragmatist distinction is conceived of as a continuum.

No doubt such a model is open to challenge. It is less important, however, than the theoretical orientation of the present study. As may have been gathered from the foregoing discussion, this is broadly pragmatist in nature and seeks to promote some accommodation between the structuralist and figurational approaches. While accepting the strictures of writers like

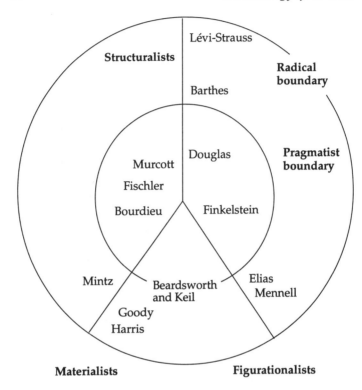

FIGURE 1.3    Relative positions of radical and pragmatist contributors
to the sociological analysis of food and eating by
theoretical orientation.

Beardsworth and Keil (1990) that integrative analyses which
incorporate materialists' interest in the biological imperatives
in food consumption are important, such a project is outside
the scope of this work. Moreover, accepting the validity of this
view should also permit of the possibility that analysis can be
conducted at a variety of levels without the encumbrance of
grand theoretical schemata. Awareness of the limitations of
theory is as important as knowledge of its potential. This said,
the form of pragmatism adopted here is pragmatic structuralism. This is because the majority of work on the sociology of
meals has been undertaken from a structuralist perspective. For
this topic at least, structuralism works – up to a point – as a
means for getting to grips with the myriad meanings that
people associate with routine acts of food consumption.

Structuralism, however, is not enough, and figurational analysis has a role to play, although its treatment in the discussion that follows might not meet with the approval of figurationalism's main champions. The overall intention is to demonstrate that different theoretical perspectives may complement rather than compete with each other. The position taken may be described, tongue in cheek, as one of 'sociological modesty', bringing concepts from the range of existing theoretical positions to bear on the sociological analysis of the meal, while recognising that these positions, taken together, are flawed, and hoping that some of the resulting embarrassment may be covered up.

# 2

## Sociologies of Domestic Dining

The previous chapter examined some of the major theoretical contributions to the study of food and eating and, in particular, the tension between 'structural' and 'materialist' perspectives. The purpose of this chapter is to review the theoretical and empirical evidence on the nature of meal-taking undertaken from a structural standpoint, namely the majority of such research, and to demonstrate the explanatory strength of the structural approach. At the same time, limitations and weaknesses in the existing corpus of knowledge will be identified.

### FUNCTION AND FEEDING

It remains a remarkable fact that whatever the broader social influences on food and eating may lead to in terms of concepts of edibility, then the taking of food is often organized around some concept of the meal, that is, on occasions when two or more people gather together primarily for the purpose of sharing food consumption. One common approach to understanding this phenomenon has been to attempt to delineate the functions of the meal and of feeding more generally, the most elegant of which is perhaps Whiteman's commentary (Whiteman, 1966; see also Knutson, 1965; de Garine, 1972; and Seymour, 1983; Firth, 1973; Farb and Armelagos, 1980; and Fieldhouse, 1986 also offer useful insights into the subject). What follows is a summary of the main features of this approach which acts as a precursor to the more detailed consideration of sociological studies of meals and meal-taking.

Food, feeding and meals can, first, demonstrate much about the nature of status differences, social groupings and relationships in society. The display and distribution of food as a means of demonstrating social status is common in many societies, and the giving of food can be an act designed to heighten the status of donors by emphasising the difference between them and the recipients of their largesse. Seymour (1983) points out that who one eats with also defines to some extent one's social group. In both the domestic and public sphere of dining, status, group membership and the quality of relationships can be revealed in a variety of ways. The kinds of food eaten with others can indicate closeness or distance in relationships. For example, a hot meal generally reflects closeness and intimacy and can be confined to immediate family and intimates (Douglas, 1975). Within the family, status and power differences according to gender can be reflected in the distribution of food (the qualities, quantities and manner of serving food). Kerr and Charles (1986) are among several researchers who have demonstrated that high meat consumption is associated with men and that women often give priority to male food preferences at the expense of their own tastes. In the workplace, class and status differences can be mirrored in the separate provision of food for managerial and related grade staff and operative workers (Batstone, 1983), although there appears to be a trend away from this form of stratification (Edwards, 1993).

Second, and following from the above, food has symbolic meanings. At the macro-social level, various forms of feasting serve to link individuals to the wider social fabric through shared understandings of cultural conventions. Thus, Christmas and Thanksgiving to some degree unite peoples and their culinary culture in shared symbolic experiences. Meals also offer opportunities for status symbolism. At one level, food can be a form of currency either in a literal sense whereby animals are exchanged for goods and services, or the giving of food as a gift is intended to elicit some reciprocal gift, service, or obligation to behave in particular ways or to repay some social debt. In the case of business lunches or 'thank you' meals, status symbolism is conveyed and reinforced by the actions of the donor in selecting what may be deemed an appropriate environment for the meal in terms of the excellence and expense of the meal.

This last point leads, thirdly, to the question of role performance (Seymour, 1983). The giving and receiving of food is never a neutral act but affords opportunities for host and guest to demonstrate appropriate behaviour as befits their roles. For a host, the meal provides opportunities to demonstrate good taste, to improve the light in which they are viewed, and to demonstrate their knowledge of what is relevant to a particular dining situation. The choice of foods by both hosts and guests similarly affords chances to demonstrate competence, not only in the manner of the choice but in the consumption of food. Mistakes over etiquette and the actual eating of food can be embarrassing, discrediting a person in the eyes of others (for example, using the 'wrong' knife or fork; employing the 'wrong' terminology – serviette instead of napkin, and so forth). Certain foods may be avoided because of the dangers they present to self-image – the eating of spaghetti or corn on the cob for example.

Self-image and the control of role performance is closely related, fourthly, to the role played by food in socialisation. Mealtimes are occasions when social groups are normally together and therefore provide opportunities for the uninitiated – particularly the young – to observe what is acceptable in terms of food-related behaviour. For children, mealtimes allow observation of what foods are routinely available for consumption and how these should be consumed – in other words, children are inculcated both formally and informally into matters of etiquette: a parent may wipe a child's mouth and face if it becomes covered with food; and food is not normally permitted to be thrown around or played with. More widely, mealtimes offer children opportunities to observe the roles played by adults – roles of cook and server, roles of main consumer, the role of 'washer-up'. For some adults, the meal may be no less an agent of socialisation. For the inexperienced in particular, attendance at 'sophisticated' meals can yield valuable clues as to the procedures and practices of formal dining.

Talking of the functions of food or of the meal is in some ways sociologically problematic in that, in sociology, 'functionalism' is a very clear theoretical position that views society as analogous to a biological organism in which the various parts of the whole function to ensure the integrity of that whole. Sociologists' objections to functionalism arise primarily from the fact that functions that tend towards conflict and destabilising the whole are seen as dysfunctional – that is as pathological and deviant rather than as a necessary expression of contrary values. The literature reviewed above does not in any general sense fall within the orbit of functionalist sociology, but nevertheless, in referring to broad functions, there is a tendency to obscure the fact that the functions of eating and meal-taking are the outcome of social processes that *are* often conflictual. Many of the so-called functions outlined above depict a uniform effect of eating upon social actors where in point of fact there are often fundamental inequalities in the extent to which (for example) food functions as a socialising agent, or is differentially stratified in terms of access. It is the underlying social processes of food preparation, cookery and consumption that have attracted most sociological interest, and it is to the key studies in this area that attention now turns.

### SOCIOLOGIES OF THE MEAL: A SHORT HISTORY

As indicated in the previous chapter, the work of social anthropologist Mary Douglas and her colleague Michael Nicod is synonymous with the sociological study of the meal, and most subsequent research owes at the very least an implicit debt to Douglas's pioneering analyses (Murcott, 1982; Delamont, 1983; Kerr and Charles, 1986; Wood, 1990; 1992b; McKie and Wood, 1991). Douglas's earliest statements on meals contain both a rejection of the 'universalist' model of food behaviour advanced by Lévi-Strauss predicated on 'binary pairs' and an explicit commitment to the understanding of social and cultural influences upon nutritional behaviour. Rather than adopting a 'top-down' approach, Douglas argues unequivocally for the theoretical grounding of the study of food and eating in localised empirical studies of dining as experienced by particular social groups. As previously suggested, however, this is not to say that Douglas's views are without certain theoretical suppositions.

In her article 'Deciphering a meal' (1975), Douglas argues that there are two contrasted food categories – meals and drinks. Meals are structured and named events (lunch, dinner and so on) whereas drinks are not. Meals are taken against a background of rituals and assumptions that include, *inter alia*, the use of at least one mouth-entering utensil per head (drinks, Douglas argues, are normally confined to mouth-touching utensils), a table, a seating order, and cultural restrictions on movement and the pursuit of alternative activities (such as reading) while seated at the table. A meal also incorporates a series of contrasts: hot and cold, bland and spiced, liquid and semi-liquid. Both meals and drinks reflect the quality of social relationships. Drinks are generally available to strangers, acquaintances, workmen *and* family. They are thus more democratic and have wider social applications. Meals, by way of contrast, are reserved for family, close friends and honoured guests. Douglas argues that there is a key relationship between meals and social distance and intimacy. 'Those we know at drinks,' she writes, 'we also know at meals' (1975: 256). The meal then expresses close friendship and family solidarity. Drinks are much less intimate. So long as this boundary matters to individuals, then the distinction between meals and drinks has meaning. This last idea may seem a somewhat inflated way of indicating that for some (perhaps many) people, such boundaries are irrelevant. Douglas, however, is simply pointing out that such boundaries are highly flexible and, in a sense, represent extremes on a continuum running from distance to intimacy along which are a variety of thresholds. This is a point taken up by Mercer (1977: 74), who outlines a continuum from hot meals, through cold meals, barbecues, cocktails and drinks, from great intimacy to minimal intimacy.

As noted above, Douglas's early empirical studies are significant to an understanding of developments in research in the sociology of eating more generally. Her colleague, Nicod, stayed as a lodger with four English working-class families for periods of up to four months, recording what was eaten and under what circumstances, and developing from this a theoretical schema for describing and analysing food behaviours. A number of assumptions and protocols were built into the research concept (Douglas, 1977). First, the English working-class diet of the time was identified as being centred upon two staple carbohydrates – potatoes and cereals – in contrast to upper and middle-class diets which made greater use of a range of cereals, beans and roots. Second, in order adequately to describe dietary habits in the families studied, Nicod developed a series of terms intended to circumscribe the contexts in which food was taken. Thus a *food event* was where food was taken without any prejudice as to whether it constituted a meal. A *meal* was a structured event, a social occasion with food governed by the aforementioned rules specifying time, place and series of actions, and was differentiated from a *snack* in that the latter was an unstructured food event (i.e. one in which no rules existed in respect of what items should be served and no strict order or sequence of the consumption of particular items was dictated) involving one or more self-contained items. Meals, in Douglas and Nicod's terms, have no self-contained items and are characterised by strict rules as to permitted combinations and sequences of foodstuffs taken.

Ignoring conventional labels, Nicod identified three types of meal: Meal A, a major meal, served around 6pm on weekdays and in the early afternoon at weekends; Meal B, a minor meal taken at 9 p.m. or 10 p.m. on weekdays and 5pm at weekends; and Meal C consisting of a biscuit and a hot drink. This last meal was a flexible component available at any time in the daily dietary cycle but most often taken both in late afternoon, on the return to the home of the principal wage-earner, and before retiring for the night. Of these three meal types, it is Meal A which is accorded the greatest analytic importance by Douglas and Nicod. A strong correspondence between the weekday evening meal and the Sunday meal was apparent. In both instances, the first course was the main course, always hot and savoury and based on a tripartite structure of potato, centre-piece (meat, fish, eggs with one or more additional vegetables) and dressing – usually gravy. The second course repeated these rules of combination except insofar as it was sweet. The staple took a cereal form (pastry, sponge), the centrepiece was often fruit and the dressing custard or cream. On Sundays and other special occasions, the second course was often followed by a third consisting of a hot drink and biscuit(s). This third course maintained similarities in rules of combination in that a biscuit has a cereal staple form enclosing a fruit or cream-type filling. In one respect, however, the pattern differed in that liquids and solids were totally separated, in contrast to other courses, and the structure was reversed insofar as the hot drink appeared in a cup or similar receptacle whereas the cold biscuit was on a plate.

Thus, according to Douglas and Nicod, are meals structured and patterned, with Meal A being an archetypal meal that sets the pattern for Meals B and C. The general pattern for meals is thus identifiable as possessing the following elements. First, the meal has certain rules of non-reversibility. In respect of staple order, potato precedes cereal in the archetypal meal, and Meal B takes the cereal staple form, usually excluding potatoes because, according to Douglas, it is the presence of the potato staple in Meal A types that lends definition to that meal, gives it its identity as it were. Second, the order of food runs from savoury to sweet and from hot to cold in terms of the principal food items consumed. Third, quantity decreases with each course as formal patterning of foodstuffs increases. In respect of the latter, Douglas sees the first course as fairly amorphous, but, as a meal progresses, this gives way to increasing geometric precision in pies, sponges and ultimately the biscuit.

What does all this mean? Douglas's central point is that research into dietary habits has traditionally failed to disengage the physiological and economic aspects of nutrition from the social in respect of family feeding:

> Criteria richer in their structural implications are used by the housewife and her family in constructing a meal . . . The housewife makes daily decisions about the elements she will need and how they can be combined. To get at the patterning of food, we should try to find the rules that guide her. (Douglas, 1977: 61)

These rules then relate to the decision-making process in eating, but what is their overall purpose? 'In the very simplicity and economy of the dietary system', Douglas says, 'the normal principles of recognition and stable structuring are at work. The housewife can serve a meal that will be acceptable to her family so long as she works within certain restrictive patternings of sequence and combination' (1977: 69).

The patterning of food therefore performs a regulatory function, encouraging family stability. There are thus very clear policy implications in Douglas's argument with respect to dietary and nutritional intervention. Douglas is concerned to emphasise, as Driver puts it, that 'it would be a waste of breath for a middle-class dietician to appear on television and advise the hard-pressed blue-collar public that stew instead of a roast and fresh fruit instead of pudding would be more economical of time or money' (1983: 172) – and, one might add, more bene-ficial to health. The real value of Douglas's early statements on the sociology of food and eating lies in the extent to which they delineate the aesthetic dimensions to meal structure and link these firmly to related implications of such structure for family constitution and nutritional policy.

Following Douglas, the next study of importance to an understanding of meals is that by Murcott (1982) of the social significance of the cooked dinner in South Wales. Murcott regards certain of Douglas's assumptions as problematic and in particular sees as limiting the unqualified treatment by the latter of the role of gender differences in food preparation and consumption. Murcott (1982) studied thirty-seven pregnant women in South Wales and found that central to the well-being of the family in dietary terms was the 'cooked dinner'. Here we find a somewhat elaborated model of Douglas's principal Meal A type. The cooked dinner, comprising meat, potatoes, at least one additional vegetable and gravy, was regarded by Murcott's sample as a 'proper meal', essential to the health and welfare of the family. It possessed structural, cyclical and symbolic fea-tures that distinguished it in the domestic dietary system from other forms of food.

Structurally, the cooked dinner was thought of as a meal in itself, was heavy not light, big not small, hot not cold. Thus, although a succession of courses was permissible, the cooked dinner as centrepiece could, in contrast to sweet-based items, stand in its own right as a meal. The cooked dinner was neces-sarily savoury, and Murcott's respondents were quite precise in describing the components that made it up. Meat was a priority, often referred to by this general term, whereas pota-toes were always specified and itemised separately from other vegetables. More detailed exploration of respondents' meanings revealed that meat always had to be fresh, not preserved, and that certain meats had common circulation – beef, lamb, pork, chicken – whereas others, notably turkey, were reserved for special occasions, and fish was not regarded as an acceptable substitute for meat in the cooked-dinner form. While potatoes were invariably a constant (roast on Sunday, usually boiled at other times), slightly more flexibility was evident in the choice of additional vegetables. Even here, however, certain rules appeared to operate. First additional vegetables were almost invariably green and from 'above ground' – peas, beans, sprouts, cabbage and occasionally broccoli and cauliflower. Second additional vegetables were prepared only in addition to these and were generally from 'below ground' – carrots, parsnips, turnips and so on. Together with meat and potatoes (which for a proper 'cooked dinner' to be constituted could not be chipped), the final ingredient necessary to the structural integrity of the cooked dinner was gravy, last in the cooking and serving sequence, and poured onto the plate after other items had been assembled. Murcott sees gravy as linking together the other items in the cooked dinner (which are normally arranged in discrete piles adjacent to each other), transforming them into a coordinated whole.

These structural features of the cooked dinner are closely linked to cyclical and symbolic qualities. Cyclically, the importance of the cooked dinner to Murcott's sample was emphasised in the fact that one day on which the cooked dinner was invariably taken was Sunday, though not on Saturday, when it was usually absent. The Sunday cooked dinner was taken around midday and usually involved more expensive and larger forms of meat and more accompanying vegetables than was common in other cooked dinners. Meat and potatoes were also characteristically roasted. Cooked dinners were not usually taken on every day of the week, but on three or four days out of seven, when they constituted the only meal of the type eaten. The importance of the cooked dinner is thus emphasised by its relative scarcity in the family dietary system, and its appearance is in the broadest sense rhythmic, confirming Douglas's notion of the weekly build-up to the archetypal Sunday lunch.

Symbolically, an important feature of cooked dinners according to Murcott is the extent to which their preparation validates women's roles in the family and marital context. The overall responsibility for domestic affairs falls to the woman of the house. There may be some parallel sharing of these responsibilities, but, where this does occur, the male adult is normally construed as simply helping. Women's responsibility for the cooked dinner extends beyond the cooking of food to include the delicate (or not so delicate) process of accommodating family food preferences and principally those of the husband or male partner. Variations in taste within the family can be accommodated by extending the range of foodstuffs included in meals – Murcott gives the example of vegetables, whereby children's preferences can be included along with those of the husband – but it is the husband's preferences which invariably take priority. Knowledge of family preferences and the manner in which they are dealt with emphasises not just the wifely or motherly role of the woman of the household but also her specific location within a particular household. The cooked dinner, as the primary and most prestigious element in the domestic dietary system, thus expresses a special relationship between the cook and those for whom the meal is cooked. More significantly yet, a woman's ability to produce a cooked dinner validates her socially and economically for, in Murcott's words, 'If a job defines how a man occupies his time during the working day, to which the wage packet provides regular testimony, proper provision of a cooked dinner testifies that the woman has spent her time in correspondingly suitable fashion . . . the cooked dinner in the end symbolizes the home itself, a man's relation to that home and a woman's place in it' (1982: 693).

At this level, Murcott extends Douglas's analysis by examining the issue of gender, something largely taken for granted by Douglas. Structurally speaking, the meal is not viewed as reflecting in a unitary fashion the sum of familial or domestic relationships, for these relationships are unequal. Murcott thus links food and eating to the pattern of power relationships within the family, and these in turn are to a very large extent gender relationships. A good many of the studies of meals that have followed Douglas and Murcott have pursued these aspects of domestic dietary culture. There are now so many of these that it is legitimate to wonder whether a point has not been reached where further additions to the canon would be repetitious (the most relevant of these to the discussion here are: Charles and Kerr, 1988; Pill and Parry, 1989; Wilson, 1989; McKie and Wood, 1991; see also the review articles by Gofton, 1989; Murcott, 1988; and Wood, 1990). The key issues are, however, important and may be summarised as follows.

First, women's relationship with food is problematic. Most

women choose what food is purchased for family consumption (Kerr and Charles, 1986, found this was true in eighty-five per cent of their cases), but this is often considered a burden rather than a power to determine the domestic dietary cycle. This is because of the need to balance a range of considerations: family tastes and preferences, food cost, variety and nutritional values among them. Women frequently subordinate their own food preferences to those of male partners, who are more often than not regarded as unadventurous – though not necessarily fussy – eaters. Women's conceptualisation of food is frequently in terms of the supposed relative energy requirements of family members. Men in particular are regarded as requiring quantity in food, particularly if they are wage-earners. Male energy needs are in any case most usually perceived as being greater than those of other family members and in particular women. Domestic labour is rarely regarded as making the same demands on energy as paid employment outside the home.

Second, the cooked dinner is a fairly ubiquitous phenomenon. While the vast majority of studies of meals have been undertaken among working-class communities and families (and often traditional working-class families at that), Charles and Kerr's (1988) work indicates that in both its conventional and more elaborate forms the cooked-dinner-type meal is a common middle-class dietary item. Women's responsibility for the cooked dinner is thus socially generalised. The cooked dinner is significant across social class, and the role of women in the preparation of meals is, on the basis of existing evidence, also widespread. Further, the preparation of food is not confined to that consumed in the home, for women are often involved in the preparation of packed lunches for children and male partners. Even here, the presence of the highly structured cooked dinner makes its mark. Batstone (1983), in his study of car workers, notes that for operatives with limited time to eat their lunch the bringing of their own 'sandwich box' allows them to maximise their lunch breaks while at the same time ensuring that personal tastes are met. Batstone writes that 'In the works canteen he has little, if any, choice of menu. But his wife – as part of the fulfilment of her role in the domestic situation – ensures that the car worker's sandwich box contains those things of which he is particularly fond . . . The sandwich box therefore provides a link with the domestic situation and,

in doing so, constitutes a form of "personalisation" of eating . . .'
(1983: 49). Though Batstone does not elaborate upon the content of workers' packed lunches, that it is sandwich-based is
suggestive of Douglas's classic carbohydrate staple – centre-
piece – dressing mode. If this is too great a supposition, then
the study by Clark and Platt (1984) of schoolchildren's packed
lunches offers harder evidence. They found that the contents of
children's packed lunches closely mirrored the 'course' structure identified by Douglas, some two-thirds of children having
a savoury plus sweet element. In the majority of cases, the
savoury element took the form of sandwiches, and there were
many instances where sandwiches included some semi-liquid
component reminiscent of the role played by gravy in cooked
dinners.

Third, the extent to which gender and food preparation (and
in particular the preparation of 'proper' meals) are firmly
cemented into familial and wider social structures can be seen
in the extent to which the 'absence' of cooked dinners or a
female to cook for men can disrupt the social fabric. What is
perceived in male eyes as a failure to produce proper cooked
dinners can lead to excesses of behaviour. Ellis (1983), in a har-
rowing report, observes that the centrality of food in marital
relationships can often lead to violence. This violence arises
because men perceive women as in some way failing in the
performance of those tasks which are regarded as properly
theirs. Many men expect domestic service to be rendered to
them exclusively, and if this service is not forthcoming in
accordance with their expectations they feel the marital con-
tract to have been broken. According to Ellis, there is a clear
expectation in many working-class subcultures that 'good'
wives have a hot meal on the table on the return of the male
wage-earner from his place of employment. Her review of the
evidence suggests that one of the principal triggers to aggres-
sive male behaviour is violation of this norm. Ellis reports the
comments of a respondent in a study by Elsey (1980): ' I was in
bed asleep and he just woke me up and said "your place is
downstairs at that cooker when I come in". That would be
about 3 or 4 am. I told him I wait until midnight and if he's not
in, I go to bed . . . he'd drag me out of bed by the hair, drag me
downstairs and make me cook him a meal' (Ellis, 1983: 167).

Ellis's argument is predicated on the observation that girls are taught from an early age to combine domestic skills with deference to the authority of males for whom they cook and serve. Male expectations of (and their attempts to control) where, when and what food will be cooked is only one aspect of this phenomenon which can extend to men seeking to organise women's time beyond cooking and serving. Ellis cites several examples of men who responded violently if women were away from the house shopping for longer than their male partner thought was reasonable. In other words, food-gender relationships have wider consequences than might be thought for an understanding of sex roles and gender inequality. To some degree, this can be seen from Coxon's study of a male cookery class (Coxon, 1983). Coxon observes that unless they are public cooks (chefs and the like), men only usually learn domestic cooking and have to practise that skill when they have no woman to cook for them. Indeed, many men are happy to boast that they cannot cook. The adult male cookery class students whom Coxon observed comprised men living for the most part in all-male households. Two types of student attended the course: absolute beginners wanting to learn basic survival cookery, and more advanced cooks who had already acquired certain skills of cookery and wanted to learn more specific skills and elaborate dishes. A large number of the 'beginners' had found themselves womanless through becoming a widower, being divorced or having lost the female relative who cooked for them (for example, their mother or sister). Seemingly the majority of these men were also heterosexual. The second group, however, comprised largely homosexual men who were unlikely to have (or have the prospect of) a female cook in the household. Coxon makes the interesting but guarded point that the composition of the first group reflected the normative priority of the female domestic role, for there were no men at the class seeking to acquire cookery skills for the purpose of becoming a component element of a 'symmetrical' family by sharing food preparation and cookery.

In teasing out these themes from the sociological literature on meal-taking, it is important not to lose sight of the fact that issues of food and family constitution are closely related to those questions of nutritional policy and responsibility (in the broadest sense) that at least partly stimulated Douglas's early work. In several of the studies cited above, a key research concern was the relationship between diet and health. Given the gendered nature of food preparation and cooking, it is unsurprising that a recurring theme in the literature is the problematic relationship which women have with respect to food provision. Not only do women have to consider the need to accommodate family tastes and ensure variety, but they also have to square these with perceived nutritional requirements. At first sight, it is difficult to reconcile what is generally cooked (cooked dinners high in fats and carbohydrates) with what is generally understood as 'healthy' eating practice. As Pill (1983) puts it, evidence from the USA suggests that mothers regard diet as important to health. The situation is much less clear as far as the UK is concerned – at least as far as formal nutritional categories are concerned.

The central issue here is that women food-providers are indeed concerned with the relationship between diet and health. The provision of cooked dinners is seen as necessary to the health of the family (Murcott, 1982). In this context, it may not be formal cultural categories that are utilised to determine what, in the eyes of both cooks and diners, is a healthy diet. As Pill's investigation of the seeming disparity between UK and US mothers' beliefs reveals, it is possible for people to operate different practical understandings of what is healthy in dietary terms. Her study of a group of working-class mothers yielded two relatively discrete orientations towards food and dietary relationships. 'Lifestyle' mothers saw illness resulting from vulnerability brought about by individual actions including those relating to diet. 'Fatalists' were more likely to view illness as deriving from external environmental influences over which they had little or no control. In dietary terms, lifestyle mothers were more likely than fatalists to mention foods that they avoided including in the family diet and to report that they made a point of including certain foods for 'health' reasons. The lifestyle mothers controlled family diet in a more planned way, whereas fatalists were more likely to tailor diet to individual needs – and in particular the needs of children. Half of Pill's sample did not perceive diet as relevant in illness causation (Pill is unclear as to whether this corresponds with the fatalist mothers), yet the majority of all women at the same time considered food to be important to keeping fit and healthy. This paradox is resolved by Pill in terms of respondents' belief that food is important for development and fuel but not in strengthening the human body against illness and disease. In terms of the moral imperatives of food consumption, 'good' or 'right' foods (good, that is, for health and well-being) were identified by both lifestyle and fatalist mothers as 'fresh'. However, fatalists more than lifestyle mothers were also much more likely to see good food as hot food. The freshness of food was defended differently by each group, fatalists favouring fresh food on the grounds of intrinsic goodness and better taste (than processed foods) and lifestyle mothers on the grounds of fresh foods containing more vitamins, and processed foods being highly suspect in terms of general effects on health. These differences within a group drawn from a similar class background are, Pill argues, evidence of the fact that the fatalist and lifestyle mothers were operating with different concepts of 'good' food and the relevance of food for health. In other words, irrespective of the validity or otherwise of nutritionists' advice, all mothers felt that they were acting in the best interests of their families when providing the domestic diet. Dietary habits therefore have to be understood in terms of wider belief systems about health.

While Pill's evidence is interesting, it is clear from a number of studies that nutritional knowledge is generally quite high, particularly among women, though this is not necessarily the same as saying that the application of this knowledge is particularly highly developed. Thomas (1980), on the basis of a 'survey of surveys', argues that while there is plenty of evidence to suggest that better nutritional knowledge is associated with positive dietary practices, there is also much evidence to the contrary. On balance, however, Thomas believes that nutritional knowledge in the form of general understandings of nutritional terms and the sources of particular nutrients has increased, albeit not dramatically. She argues that two factors are important in influencing the application of sound nutritional knowledge to dietary practice. The first is the extent to which educational programmes involve participants in the understanding of these relationships. The second is the salience that nutrition and dietary relationships assume in particular contexts – for example, Thomas cites evidence that shows knowledge of calorific values to be higher among dieters than non-dieters and among the obese as compared to the non-obese. In more general terms,

Thomas concurs with the arguments outlined earlier, citing a 1978 survey to the effect that the main factors influencing a housewife's food choice are (a) her desire to appear a caring wife and mother; (b) the time available to her; (c) the money available to her; and (d) influences from her own upbringing and the type of environment in which she lives. The clear implication, then, is the one outlined by Douglas, namely that nutritional policy and education need to take account of structures of culinary value, and, as Murcott and subsequent researchers have demonstrated, this in turn is related to the structure of power relations in the family and wider society. The specific upshot of the dietary studies of social nutritionists and sociologists is that even where, perhaps, the nutritional knowledge of (women) food-preparers and cooks is sound, it is not always possible to implement this in a familial context because social norms and conventions demand a more pragmatic approach to family feeding.

Thomas's point about the application of nutritional knowledge being closely related to educational programmes and contexts of especial importance to individuals is important here. Thomas is mainly concerned with formal education programmes and specific dietary states (e.g. obesity). However, 'education' can come in many forms. Several recent studies have, with varying degrees of explicitness, shown that media messages arising from general food advertising or from news coverage of the many 'food scares' of the late 1980s generate confusion and anger among those women who have responsibility for family diet. McKie and Wood (1991) (see also Wilson, 1989; Beardsworth, 1990; McKie, Wood and Gregory, 1993), in a study of working-class women in north-east England, found that attempts by the food industry and other sources to 'educate' the eating public were experienced by many women as a form of pressure that took no account of family preferences for conventional fare. Furthermore, such messages were often regarded as conflicting, making it more difficult for women to cater for their family. This conflict was compounded by the many food scares at the time, relating to salmonella in eggs, listeria, 'mad cow disease' and botulism in the puree used to flavour hazelnut yoghurt, incidents which served to heighten women's awareness of food-health relationships and instil in them concern about the 'correctness' of their dietary practices.

Nutritional knowledge then need not be acquired formally. Informal pressures arising from media advice (irrespective of the source of such advice) can be equally powerful in pressurising women as they seek to cater for their families. What is clear is that, notwithstanding 'folk' beliefs in the nutritional and health value of cooked dinners, perceptions of what constitutes 'nutritional knowledge' are a cause of concern for many women. However, the very concept of the 'cooked dinner' obscures the fact that in subordinating their own tastes to those of their menfolk and children, many women not only eschew their own personal tastes and understanding of nutritional imperatives, but often participate less in the dominant domestic dietary experience. Kerr and Charles (1986) found that very high consumption of meat was almost totally confined to men while very low meat consumption was associated primarily with women and children, although social class differences were important here, with professional/management males consuming less meat than others and manual unskilled workers evidencing the highest consumption. Several other studies have shown that women often go without food, particularly in families where there is financial hardship. Women's problems are compounded further in respect of food because, as a result of societal pressures, they are closely preoccupied with the relationship between food and body weight and image (Charles and Kerr, 1988; McKie, Wood and Gregory, 1993). The dominant domestic dietary system – or at least the cooked dinner at its heart – is not conducive to the sylph-like frame expected of 'desirable' women. At the same time, it is clear from the work of those like Wilson (1989) that women have much greater capacity for dietary change than men. The frustrations involved in the tension between personal food preferences and family feeding are thus heightened, and beliefs about what is good for the family in terms of food consumption are constantly tested against women's perceptions of 'good nutrition' and their personal, preferred, ways of eating.

### DOMESTIC DINING: THE LIMITATIONS OF STRUCTURE?

In any reasoned consideration, the evidence examined in the preceding section should be adequate testimony to the sensitivity of structuralist analysis to the meanings that social actors attach to acts of food consumption. Yet a variety of academic, quasi-academic and lay objections, other than the theoretical issues considered in the previous chapter, remain to be addressed. Five in particular are important. The first objection is that meal-taking as the primary vehicle for consumption is in decline. The second points to the methodological limitations of the qualitative research so far discussed in this chapter, pointing out that many studies are of traditional working-class families and households, and that the findings of such research cannot be generalised to all classes (a similar view, it will be recalled, is advanced by Charsley, 1992, in the context of Douglas' work – see Chapter 1, pp. 13–14). A third objection is that greater equality between the sexes means that qualitative studies of meal-taking among the working class exaggerate the extent to which women are the main providers and preparers of food, and underplay the extent to which these activities are now much more democratically organised. The fourth routine complaint concerns the extent to which regional, national and international variations in food consumption are underplayed in structural analyses. A final objection relates to the perceived failure of structural analyses to acknowledge the role of healthier eating in society and concomitant attempts to modify diet, the argument being, again, that the 'cooked dinner' of meat and two vegetables is, increasingly, in decline. Each of these will now be considered in turn.

### The Death of the Meal

In her review of the (then) available evidence, Thomas wrote: 'Although the emphasis on the importance of particular meals may have changed, the UK is still predominantly a country of three meals a day with snacks' (1982: 211). Among the observations cited by Thomas are those from a 1978 survey by the Kraft company which suggested that eighty per cent of men and seventy-three per cent of women responding to the survey claimed that the entire family sat down to a meal every day, compared with twenty per cent of women and twelve per cent of men who stated that this only occurred at the weekend (Thomas, 1982: 219). In terms of the long march of history, 1978 is, of course, fairly recent. Nevertheless, Thomas's observation is important if only for understanding the subsequent (and

now seemingly almost perennial) tendency for commentators
to proclaim the death of the meal – a trend most evident in the
press.

For example, an article by Marshall (1991: 35) in *The Independent* newspaper reported a survey by The Henley Centre
that purported to show that 'The dining room, the dining table
and the family meal are going the way of cooked breakfasts
and high teas . . . increasingly within families, people eat on
their own, even when others are at home'. The trend is not,
however, as dramatic as might first appear. What the Henley
Centre in fact found was that one in four people eats a main
meal on their own most days in the week and the main reason
for this is related to time factors. Specifically, mothers have less
time to fulfil their 'traditional' role because they are at work,
and 'teenagers and husbands who used to consume it [food]
are pursuing their own leisure interests or getting home later
because of commuting time'. In the *Sunday Telegraph* of 28
March 1993, Nicholas Coleridge similarly sounds the death
knell for Sunday lunch. Coleridge too identifies time as a key
factor in the decline of the 'traditional' Sunday lunch – specifically the effort-reward relationship implied by the cooking of a
joint against that required to prepare simpler food. Also among
the culprits, Coleridge identifies modern adult attitudes, suggesting that the 'traditional roles played by the adults of the
house have been forgotten. Most modern women have not a
clue how long it takes to roast different meats' (1993: I).

In both these pieces, there is an unselfconscious sexism
which recognises the pivotal role of women in the preparation
of meals without ever challenging the notion. Both pieces add
up to very little, however. Nor do academic pronouncements
on this subject, for it is not only journalists who have prophe-
sied the end of the meal. Fischler (1980: 946–7) proclaims 'the
empire of snacks', arguing that the institutionalised, ritualised
act of meal-taking is on the decline while 'snacking' and 'nibbling' is on the increase. This notion fits well with the popular
image of eating in Western societies becoming more a matter of
grazing than feeding. Fischler refers to an American survey of
the late 1970s which revealed that urban middle-class families
could have as many as twenty 'food contacts' a day; three-
quarters of such families did not eat breakfast together; the
evening meal could take place as infrequently as three times a

week; and 'The daily three-meal pattern, although mentioned as a valid rule by almost all the subjects, is no longer a reality' (1980: 946). The lack of clarity in this last statement does not prevent Fischler from asserting with great authority that nibbling is the new order and that while this seems to be less of the case in Europe, there is an increasing tendency towards snacking. This was in 1980, and Fischler argues that:

> It is therefore legitimate to diagnose, in the mainstream of Western, urban, industrial societies, a process of disaggregation and disintegration affecting the social dimension of eating habits and the cultural framework shaping them. Meals are being increasingly eroded by or reduced to snacks. Eating is becoming less of a social, and more of a strictly individual practice. (Fischler, 1980: 947)

Even by sociologists' standards, this generalisation is breathtaking. Writing more or less at the same time as Fischler, Bourdieu (1984) did not appear to identify the same trends in France. Nor, given the weight of evidence so far considered in this chapter, does 'snacking' appear to have *overtaken* meals as the dominant mechanism for food consumption.

In their UK study conducted during the 1980s, Charles and Kerr (1988) found that women in low-income families were most inclined to express a frustrated inability to feed their household 'properly', that is in terms of providing a 'proper meal containing meat of a relatively high social status' (1988: 173). Charles and Kerr's study is notable for the large number of families from different social classes, but even they found that most in their sample ate three meals a day of which one was ideally a 'proper' meal. Moreover, 'The timing of the main meal depended on when everyone could be at home to eat, and in families with young children this usually depended on the man's hours of work' (1988: 180). Charles and Kerr are emphatic in their conclusion that across all social classes represented in their sample, women regarded the 'proper meal' as central to the family food system. Charles and Kerr's evidence suggests that 'nibbling' and 'snacking' has yet to displace meal-taking as the basis for domestic, family, food consumption, a view also supported by the work of Dare (1988). In her study, Dare analysed sixty-three food diaries completed by working-and middle-class couples in west London and found that, contrary to (popular) survey results, the supposed trend towards snacking and away from the formal family meal was not greatly in evidence. Some seventy per cent of meals in Dare's study were eaten *en famille*, thirteen per cent were consumed separately, while fourteen per cent of meals entailed children eating separately from their parents (interestingly, this last trend was slightly more evident in middle-class homes where the majority of academics, journalists and other public commentators are reared!). Perhaps most significant of all, however, was Dare's finding that '80% of snacks, which are predominantly convenience food, were eaten together as a family' (1988: 152).

### Class Differences

The evidence against the decline of the meal as the mainspring of domestic food provision and consumption also suggests that the 'cooked dinner' is a fairly ubiquitous phenomenon across all social classes. It would be wrong, however, to pretend that there are not social-class variations in food consumption. In this respect, the cooked dinner functions as an ideal type that is to a greater or lesser extent flexible but not entirely mutable in both structure and content. Clearly, the cooked-dinner 'model' is a valid concept for analysing meal forms and what may be termed 'variations on a theme'. Some of these variations might arise because of 'external' influences that act upon food consumers, for example the availability of foods. Availability itself may relate in turn to agricultural factors – plenty or shortage – or to institutionalised forms of class-based taste preferences as suggested by Barthes (1973) and Bourdieu (1984). Availability might also be a function of accessibility. In social-class terms, the relationship between occupational class and income is important here (Charles and Kerr, 1988).

Class is thus an important differentiator when it comes to analysing food consumption. Class affects access to foods, the development of culinary cultures and concepts of taste, and ultimately, when taken with environmental factors and food availability, the structures of dining that emerge in any given context. Even the arch-materialist Harris (1986: 16–17) while acknowledging that food preferences and avoidances stem from some favourable balance of practical costs and benefits, acknowledges that this favourable balance is not necessarily shared equally by all. It is not easy to separate matters of taste and preference in food choice in circumstances of relative financial security from those in cases of financial constraint. As Bourdieu (1984) argues, 'coarse' taste can persist even in conditions of relative financial security, where some choice exists in the enactment of dietary change. Furthermore, it makes sense to acknowledge that changing food patterns over time, and diverse food preferences at any given moment in time, may disguise enduring though varied key structures. Thus, Douglas (1975) claims that middle-class diet is more varied and has greater range than that of the working class, a view supported with greater authority (Douglas offers little evidence for her assertion) by Mennell, Murcott and van Otterloo (1992). It is reasonable to assume, given the historical evidence (Burnett, 1979; Mennell, 1985), that such variations are the contemporary manifestation of long-standing social inequalities that have had a number of different forms. An interesting and not entirely irrelevant aside on this phenomenon in a historic, micro-social context, is offered by Gibson and Smout (1988: 35–8), who studied historical evidence of food and eating at the Court of James VI and Anne of Denmark. The court had three kitchens, one cooking for the King, one for the Queen and one for the Court at large. Meals were held in three or four rooms but access to particular types of food was dictated by status within the Court and reflected in formal food allowances. These formal allowances were complemented by formal and informal channels for passing left-over food ('rests') down the hierarchy.

Forms of inequality shift over time, yet structures can persist. In his study of food statistics, Hornsby-Smith (1984) reports that over nearly half a century, the distribution of household expenditure on five main categories of foodstuff (meat, fish and eggs; dairy products and fats; fruit and vegetables; cereals; all other foods) has remained remarkably constant. Furthermore, shifts in the allocation of expenditure have tended to be more within particular food groups than between them. Thus, in the period 1961–80, coffee consumption tripled, partially substituting for tea, but bacon and egg consumption declined relative to breakfast cereal consumption. These general trends disguise class differences. Higher-income groups are more likely to drink coffee than tea, purchase pork in preference to lamb, and spend more on wholemeal bread and fresh fruit and vegetable produce, suggesting, according to Hornsby-Smith, that 'they can afford to be more concerned with the relationship between diet and health than other groups' (1984: 208).

This may well be the case, but the key point here is the extent to which the basic structures of consumption have remained relatively firm over time, with variation by class exhibiting a pattern of close substitution. Charles and Kerr (1988) are again instructive in this respect, relating the purchasing elements of food consumption to their respondents' views of proper meal provision. They write:

> The importance of preserving proper meal consumption in some form, even if it was less frequent and of lower status, ran through all the comments of women managing on low incomes and most of them felt that as long as a cooked dinner could be provided daily they were eating properly and adequately, although not as well as they would like. (1988: 174)

Clearly then, inter- and intra-class differences in food preferences and consumption may be demonstrated, but on balance these reflect a bias towards maintaining structure. Class inequalities themselves are an important source of differentiation or variation on the theme of ritualised, structured dining. The distinctiveness of class-based food consumption that does not disrupt the overall theme of structure in dining is supported indirectly by Tomlinson and Warde (1993), who suggest that survey evidence has tended to show that the working-class diet is, in nutritional terms, relatively inadequate. In terms of symbolic aspects of inequality and difference in consumption, Tomlinson and Warde's analysis of Family Expenditure Survey data for 1968 and 1988 leads them to assert that (a) there are persistent class-based trends to purchase particular types of food irrespective of price changes; and (b) though smaller in size in 1988 than in 1968, the manual working class retains distinctive dietary practices supportive of specific class tastes and cultures.

The general import of such evidence lies in the extent to which it supports, however weakly, the view of food preparation and consumption as a structured activity with variations in structure being enabled and constrained by factors like income available for expenditure on food, and class-based tastes. If Hornsby-Smith (1984) is to be believed, then variations on the central theme according to class take place within food categories, and it is not unreasonable to infer as a working hypothesis that constraints of income give rise to the phenomenon of close substitution in dietary practice the less money there is available to spend on food. This leads to archetypal meal structures (for example, roast beef and all the trimmings) being diluted either on a product basis (replacing beef with a 'lesser' meat) or on the basis of some other criterion (for example, cheaper cuts of the same kind of meat – perhaps brisket instead of silverside in the case of beef). What is unclear from the research of writers like Tomlinson and Warde (1993) is the extent to which distinctive working-class patterns of eating follow, as Bourdieu (1984) suggests, a tendency from choice to 'trade down' in food consumption within food categories. Indeed, a fair proportion of the evidence suggests that even when the working class cannot afford to, it aspires to 'good' food in the sense of quality cuts of meat, fresh vegetables and so on. Clearly then, until such a time as further evidence becomes available to clarify this issue, it would be unwise to associate a distinctive British working-class diet with a tendency to 'eat down' in conditions of relative financial security.

### Gender

One of the most frequently vaunted 'common-sense' objections to the micro-sociological studies of women's roles in food purchase and preparation is that greater marital and family democracy means that men now play a much larger role in these activities than would be suggested by the evidence discussed earlier. The wider historical dimensions to these kinds of argument are considered expertly elsewhere (see especially Mennell, Murcott and van Otterloo, 1992). If, because of methodological objections (for example, sample size, type of community considered), the studies examined earlier still fail to convince, then there are others that might persuade. In the study by Dare (1988) referred to earlier, it was evident to the author that:

> The mean time per meal . . . reveals quite starkly the unequal division of labour and the way convenience foods may play a role in reducing women's work

time. Breakfasts and snacks are meals featuring a
high proportion of convenience foods, where time is
somewhat less unequally divided between family
members, suggesting such meals are prepared by
household members other than the woman. Yet other
meals reveal the same high proportion of convenience
foods used with a grossly unequal division of time.
Indeed in preparing Sunday lunch women spend
14 times longer than men and children combined.
(Dare, 1988: 149–50)

The common-sense concept of greater marital and family
democracy in the performance of household tasks including
food purchase and preparation takes a further knock from a
1993 study by the Mintel market research organisation reported
extensively in the national press (see for example Erlichman,
1993: 6). The key point to emerge from this report was that
around eighty-five per cent of working women said they were
entirely responsible for cooking their household's main meal.
The point is, of course, that even where male and female partners are in paid work, responsibility for food preparation tends
to fall to the woman. Evidence at least slightly contrary to these
trends does exist. Charles and Kerr (1988) found a significant
class variation in the gendered division of domestic labour. In
both shopping and cooking, Charles and Kerr note, 'men in
classes I and II were much more likely to help out with these
tasks than their working-class counterparts' (1988: 176). The
term 'help out' may be significant in this context, as it seems to
lend support to the earlier noted phenomenon that where men
do become involved in domestic activities such as cooking, it is,
at best, in a half-hearted and ancillary way. On the whole, the
case for greater equality in gender relationships within the
home has yet to be adequately demonstrated, and any assertion
to the contrary has to be considered sceptically.

### Regional, National and International Variations
Aside from class and gender, a number of other potential
variations are sometimes cited as undermining the case for
viewing the UK domestic diet as centred on relatively immu-
table and structured acts of meal-based food consumption.
Regional differences in food-consumption patterns persist,

though Hornsby-Smith (1984) cites evidence to suggest that these are less marked than in the past. However, some evidence at least (Allen, 1968; Hughes, 1977) supports the view that, despite long-standing regional food differences within the UK, a national 'food culture' has existed for some time with such differences representing, once again, instances of variations on a central theme.

International evidence is also suggestive of the general accuracy of the view of meals as central to domestic dining systems, as well as highlighting for some countries the structural qualities and social relationships attendant on acts of food consumption. As early as the 1940s, Bennett, Smith and Passin (1942) in a study of food habits in several areas of southern Illinois found that, in all the locations studied, food consumption centred on three staples: potatoes, beans and pork. The authors term this the core diet and note that around the core was, first, a secondary core, consisting of many foodstuffs that had recently become available for purchase from local stores; and, second, a peripheral diet of infrequently used foods outside of the core and secondary core. All three of these concepts are used in similar form by Jerome (1980) in a study of the southern American diet in Milwaukee. Jerome charts content variations found in meals and snacks for all of 'normal' weekday meals, 'Sunday dinner' and festive meals (for example, Thanksgiving). Again, emphasis is placed on the scope and potential for close substitution of foodstuffs in a core model of what respondents saw as 'appropriate' forms of dietary consumption. Jerome argues that the dietary order consists of core and staple items; secondary core items, which are added to or substituted for items in the core as circumstances and contexts vary; and peripheral dietary items, which are those items used infrequently, including ceremonial foods.

In a much more complex series of studies of Italian-American diet in Philadelphia, Judith Goode and various colleagues have elaborated empirical examples of the 'theme and variations' model of food consumption centred on the meal. Goode, Theophano and Curtis (1984) place particular emphasis on the concepts of meal formats and meal cycles. Meal formats are 'model structures for arranging dishes in course sequences or in synchronic presentation within a meal. Courses can consist of single dishes or multiple dishes. Certain dishes must go together, others must be separated. Some dishes must follow others' (1984: 72). Through careful analysis of meal formats, Goode, Theophano and Curtis are able to relate variations in the selection of different meal formats to meal cycles (food-consumption patterns over time), community values and activity patterns of households, building up a many-layered picture of the interrelationships between the role of food in people's lives and other aspects of the social order.

These kinds of study are conceptually useful for elaborating the parameters of the structural model of meal-based food consumption, but they also highlight some of the limitations of such analysis, focusing as they do on food consumption in two similar countries – the USA and the UK. It is not possible easily to generalise structural models to other kinds of society, and the temptation must be avoided. Nevertheless, the value of the structuralist model to elaboration of dietary preference in the contexts so far studied is considerable. There is no *de facto* reason for supposing that similar models cannot be used to analyse consumption in other kinds of society. Befu (1974) offers some insight into how this might be achieved in a study of meal provision in Japan, a highly traditional non-Western society that evidences considerable industrialisation.

Befu (1974) offers an analysis of dinner entertainment in Japan in order to illustrate how cultural assumptions are integral to meal provision. Even if the facilities of the home are adequate to the task, the home is regarded as a private sanctuary, so the Japanese prefer to entertain business associates at a Japanese (as opposed to Western) restaurant. The Japanese restaurant – or ryootei/ryooriya – is preferred for several reasons, all connected to the Japanese desire to honour guests. First, people sit on the floor on cushions, unlike in a Western restaurant. Diners also have a private room for their entertaining, and, whereas in Western restaurants service employees such as waiters and waitresses are effectively non-persons, in ryootei servers (who are always women) are an integral part of the entertainment, expected to participate in conversation (although this participation is expected to be passive – unless the woman concerned is a geisha – confined to speaking only when spoken to and not initiating conversation). Second, the ordering of food in a ryootei is done by the host alone, usually by telephone beforehand, and the bill is paid secretly so guests know nothing of either individual or total costs. This functions, Befu argues, to obscure the pecuniary aspects of dinner entertainment and create an atmosphere of homeliness. A corollary of this is that ryootei lend themselves to creating a social environment conducive to group cohesion – at least among the Japanese – since all have the same dishes and there is an emphasis on the common sharing of experience, unlike in Western restaurants, where individual choice is possible. Third, an important rule to be followed in the dinner entertainment of a small party is to centre the conversation of the group on a single topic. Breaking up is socially unacceptable and insulting to guests, as is any attempt to change the topic or a demonstration of disinterest. Finally, sake is served in ryootei and not normally in Western restaurants. Sake-drinking is an important ritual, sake allegedly being a sacred beverage. Befu suggests that the communal functions of sake-drinking are deeply embedded in ordinary dinner entertainments in Japan.

The rules of sake-drinking are complex. Pouring of the drink is not by oneself but for each other, a symbolic gesture indicating that each person is at the service of the other. Since sake cups are small, constant surveillance is necessary in order to ensure that cups are replenished. At the same time, however, it is required of social etiquette that while filling sake cups, guests remain absorbed in conversation. When sake is poured, Befu tells us, the owner of a cup should hold it in their hand rather than leaving it on the table, so as to avoid the implication that the pouring of sake is being ignored. If a guest has had sufficient sake and wishes to accept a little more but not a full cup, then the cup must be moved higher and higher to prevent overfilling. Good hosts do not necessarily respect their guests' wishes, and the bottle containing the sake may also be lifted higher and higher. There is, then, no socially acceptable way of refusing sake without committing a social *faux pas*. Status is intimately bound up with sake-drinking. Befu notes that:

> Etiquette requires that the host first pour *sake* for the guest, the host symbolically being the servant of the guest, and that the guest then reciprocate. It also

requires that if a person of lower status wishes to exchange drinking with a person of higher status, the former first pours for the latter, and then the latter reciprocates. Also, if their seats are far apart, as they may be in a large party, the junior person is required to come to the senior person and ask him for the privilege of pouring sake for him. (Befu, 1974: 200)

Befu's study highlights the way in which meals are structured around social interaction, reflecting gendered serving roles and status differences in dining parties. Meal structure is an important element of the essential communality of Japanese dining in this context: a multitude of dishes are provided that reflect and reinforce this communality, but at the same time inequalities between members of the group are seemingly not reflected, as in Western domestic dining, in differential access to certain types of food; and, it may be supposed, this is because the participants in such dining are all male.

### Eating Differently

One source of variation often cited as undermining the general validity of structural analyses of the meal is the supposed move in many Western societies towards 'healthier eating', a trend that has diluted the significance of the cooked dinner of meat, two vegetables and gravy in the diet of the general population. The problematic nature of definitions of 'healthy eating' makes for conceptual difficulties in discussing this issue. As writers like Murcott (1982), Charles and Kerr (1988) and Pill (1983) show, in many working-class subcultures, a healthy diet and healthy eating are construed in terms of the quantity of food and the appearance of food in the form of the cooked dinner. Further, the many and frequent reports from the medical profession and other nutritionally concerned bodies and individuals that bombard the public are indicative of the extent to which, in scientific terms at least, the British remain a nation of unhealthy eaters.

Ironically, one of the reasons why dietary change of certain sections of the population is difficult to achieve may well lie in the often conflicting nutritional advice which people receive from media sources (McKie and Wood, 1991). Thus, even where socio-economic circumstances do permit of choice and flexibility in food purchase, preparation and consumption, confusion about the 'correct' route to a healthier diet can encourage continuing reliance on trusted dietary forms and contents. Nevertheless, there is some evidence that in circumstances where dietary choice is possible, there exists greater scope for flexibility in meal content than is evident from studies of working-class subcultures. Charles and Kerr (1988: 195) found that women in higher social classes attached less importance to meat as part of meals than women in lower social classes. Among the higher social classes, meals were often egg- or cheese-based, and included beans and other pulses 'without this being felt as a social deprivation' (1988: 195). Charles and Kerr also note that:

> Spaghetti and other pasta and rice based meals were more frequent and took the place of the traditional meat and two veg., whereas in more working-class households the *structure* of the proper meal was maintained even though the constituent elements might not be 'proper'. (Charles and Kerr, 1988: 195)

Interestingly, it could be argued that the substitution of eggs, cheese, pasta and rice for meat and two vegetables is itself a reflection of the tendency to preserve the structure of the meal (though not the 'cooked dinner') through the inclusion of variant carbohydrate staples and protein centrepieces. The process of close substitution is not all that different in this case from that in economically disadvantaged households where cheaper meats or cuts of meat are used instead of those deemed more appropriate to maintaining the structure of the cooked dinner.

Remarkably little is known about the diversity of dietary practices followed by those who claim to be healthy eaters. Rather more is known about what might be regarded as the logical extension of healthy eating practices within the dominant food culture – that is, vegetarianism. One of the most compelling and influential studies of contemporary vegetarianism is that offered by Twigg (1983), who argues that vegetarianism in the West is an explicit food ideology that requires individuals following a vegetarian diet to step outside the normal pattern of eating. In contrast, in societies such as India, vegetarianism is bound up with the caste system: high-caste Hindus do not eat meat, and vegetarianism is linked to a whole series of other prohibitions and taboos that form part of a hierarchical system of grading according to concepts of purity and status. Vegetarianism in this context is a normative feature of the social structure whereas in the West it is not, and to become a vegetarian is often to invite a negative or at least uncertain response from non-vegetarians.

Twigg notes that vegetarianism is very diverse: people who become vegetarians do so for many different reasons which, however, can be grouped under four primary headings – health, animal welfare concerns, economic and ecological preoccupations, and spiritual reasons. Further, one of the main characteristics of vegetarianism is that it rarely occurs alone but is usually linked to a complex of other beliefs. These views are confirmed by empirical research. Both Dwyer et al. (1974) and Beardsworth and Keil (1992) found the vegetarians they studied to advance a variety of reasons as to their conversion, though in both studies there was an emphasis on the interrelatedness of motivations to become vegetarians and of the relationship of vegetarianism to other belief systems. In terms of straightforward categories, Dwyer et al. (1974) found that the major reasons for being vegetarian among their sample of 212 respondents were health (thirty-five per cent); ethical and moral considerations (twenty-five per cent); metaphysical beliefs (fourteen per cent); ecological concerns (eight per cent); and food preference reasons (also eight per cent). A 1989 MORI poll in the UK discovered the principal motivations for being vegetarian to be disapproval of animal husbandry (sixty-one per cent); moral rejection of animal slaughter (fifty-eight per cent); dislike of the taste and texture of the meat (thirty-eight per cent); and health concerns (forty-nine per cent) (Beardsworth and Keil, 1991a). The MORI poll results are indicative of the multiple-layered nature of the reasons for becoming a vegetarian. The diversity of vegetarian culinary culture is well captured by Beardsworth and Keil (1991a; 1991b) whose studies repay more detailed consideration.

Beardsworth and Keil conducted interviews with thirty-nine female and thirty-seven male vegetarians. Considerable variations in eating patterns were revealed. Four of the sample were occasional meat-eaters defining themselves as vegetarians, meat consumption occurring most often when no vegetarian options were available, or in order to avoid social embarrassment (Beardsworth and Keil, 1991b: 20). A further eighteen respondents were vegans who tried to avoid all animal foods. Between these two extremes in ascending order of dietary self-discipline were fish-eaters (nineteen respondents), lacto-ovo vegetarians (eating eggs, dairy products and rennet-free cheeses; twenty-six respondents); and lacto-vegetarians (eating dairy produce and rennet-free cheeses; nine respondents). In simple terms, forty-three respondents were vegetarian for moral and spiritual reasons, thirteen for health reasons, nine for taste reasons, one for ecological reasons, three each for a combination of health and taste, and moral and taste reasons, and two for health and moral reasons. Conversion to vegetarianism occurred in various ways. For many, the process was gradual, marked by a number of stages involving changes in diet. In other cases, conversion was more violent, often triggered by some memorable experience. In both gradual and abrupt conversion, however, it was usually the case that vegetarians moved along a vegetarian scale of denial to their current position, giving up meat first, followed by fish and then other products. Beardsworth and Keil (1991b: 20) propose a six-point vegetarian scale running from meat-eating at one extreme, through fish-eating, egg-eating, consumption of dairy produce and consumption of rennet-free cheese, to consumption of vegetable-derived products. This corresponds broadly to Twigg's conceptualisation of the process of becoming and being a vegetarian, as does Beardsworth and Keil's (1991a) finding that for many vegetarians and vegans, meat is associated with death, the dead, and decay – the very opposite of what meat represents in the dominant culinary culture.

Twigg (1983) makes this last point emphatically, pointing to the symbolic potency of meat as possessing associations with strength, passion, aggression and sexuality. The dominant (meat-eating) culture places constraints on these animalistic qualities of humans, for example by forbidding or stigmatising the consumption of raw and bloody food. Further, controls on meat consumption have been (and continue to be) placed on certain groups. Victorian health manuals initiated a long-standing if now largely defunct practice of recommending a reduction in meat consumption for pregnant women, instead encouraging the consumption of light and delicate foods that mirrored women's own presumed delicacy. A similar ideological constraint persists in the treatment of invalids and the sick, who are supposed not to be aided by the consumption of 'strong foods'. Similarly, educationalists of the Victorian era recommended a low-meat diet for adolescent males as a means of countering masturbation. For Twigg, the dominant food hierarchy consists of red meat at the apex, followed by poultry and then fish. At this point, the 'vegetarian boundary' is reached, and eggs and cheese are the next items in the descending order of status, at which point the 'vegan boundary' is crossed. The hierarchy continues downwards with fruit, leaf vegetables, root vegetables and cereals occupying bottom position. Vegetarians are often seen as eating 'down' this hierarchy and reversing its ideological connotations such that it is those items nearer the bottom, not the top, that are seen as healthy, vital and life-giving.

The same is true to some degree of health-food users. As a category distinct from (but sometimes overlapping with) various categories of vegetarians, health-food users should, themselves, be seen as in some cases separate from those who merely claim to be committed to 'healthy eating', if only because the latter term is, as has been shown, difficult to define in any objective sense. Kandel and Pelto (1980) argue that people who define themselves as health-food users eat less animal flesh and fewer processed and convenience foods, pursuing their diets for spiritual, physical and psychological reasons, often also believing that their eating patterns are more compatible with a healthy environment and balanced ecology. In this sense, the distinction between 'serious' health-food users and various categories of vegetarian is barely worth worrying about. Of greater research interest is that category of healthy eaters who, in terms of personal consumption, make simpler modifications to their diet. According to Beardsworth and Keil (1991a), social surveys at the end of the 1980s suggested that vegetarians of one type or another constituted around three per cent of the population. The number of 'healthy eaters' is probably much greater. However, it would be premature to argue that Britain's cooked-dinner culture is being undermined by trends towards healthy eating, whatever form that eating might take.

Indeed, few of the objections to the structuralist analysis of

meals considered in this chapter appear to be especially persuasive. They look less so in the light of evidence pertaining to
dining outside of the home. This assertion will be developed
further in the next chapter, where discussion of the themes and
issues raised here are elaborated in the context of public dining
– 'dining out'. At the same time, analysis of dining out as a
social activity will be shown to offer a further context for the
elaboration of relationships between structuralist approaches
to the study of food and other, complementary, theoretical
perspectives.

# 3

---

# *Dining Out*

---

Sociologists have, for the most part, neglected dining out in their analyses of food-culture relationships. With the exception of the work of Mennell (1985) and Finkelstein (1989), there are few substantive commentaries on the topic (though the impressionistic study by Driver (1983) could be legitimately cited as an important contribution to the subject). The approach adopted to the study of dining out in this chapter is a little idiosyncratic. The first part of the chapter carries on where the previous two left off, by offering a résumé and discussion of how dining out may be viewed from a broadly structuralist perspective. The remainder of the chapter is given over to considering how certain other theoretical concepts bear on this discussion and issues raised elsewhere in the present work. In adopting this approach, the intention is to reinforce the view that analysis of dining out can offer useful pointers to how a broader theoretical milieu may be constituted for the purposes of widening research considerations in the sociological analysis of food and eating beyond the existing, relatively narrow, focus of interest.

## MEAL STRUCTURE AND DINING OUT

Mars and Nicod have written that 'the restaurant menu lies outside the ordinary daily round of food-taking and it must not be confused with menus from the family food system' (1984: 52). Evidence suggests that they are wrong and that the public provision of food is very closely linked to domestic family food systems. Although the hotel and catering (or, as the preferred term now has it, 'hospitality') industry is relatively heterogeneous in terms of the different ways in which food is provided, the dining-out market is, in the main, one of small extremes and a large centre. At one extreme are those establishments that provide various forms of haute cuisine and specialist foods and styles for which there is a limited market. At the other extreme are the humble street-corner take-away food shops offering the most basic foodstuffs. In the middle, so-called popular catering covers a multitude of establishments including everything from steak houses, carveries and most Chinese and Indian restaurants, to fast-food restaurants and chain restaurants offering speciality cuisines such as pizza and pasta. According to the National Westminster Bank (1991), in 1989 there were some 231,750 commercial catering outlets in Britain and some 5,273 million meals were served in total. In the non-commercial sectors of the industry, some 2,987 million meals were served in around 72,610 outlets. The average spend on a meal in the same year was £5.46, up from £3.11 in 1981. All these figures are probably underestimates. While dining out remains, for many, a special occasion marked by specific rituals, for others it is an increasingly routine activity that is integral to daily patterns of existence (Wood, 1992b).

As a means of illustrating the general point that the forms of public dining are indeed influenced heavily by domestic dietary systems, it is instructive first to consider the work of Delamont (1983) on wedding meals. Delamont begins from the premise that wedding meals are important ritual events, and wedding meals convey important messages about marriage and the role of women in society. To some extent, the menus chosen for wedding meals are a matter of 'tradition', but there are a number of external influences which act upon societal conventions about 'appropriate' foodstuffs for wedding meals. These are women's magazines and cookery books (which are directed towards women in general, irrespective of marital status) and magazines and periodicals specifically devoted to the topic of weddings, and books on marriage and wedding etiquette. Significantly, Delamont argues, the bride does not cook at her own wedding; she is a guest. The reception menu is the concern of the bride's mother, or a caterer under the mother's guidance, and is paid for by the bride's father. The wedding meal is usually an expensive occasion and, according to the media sources examined by Delamont, there are only two choices of cook – the mother or paid outsider (caterer) – and three possible, acceptable, locations for the wedding reception: the bride's family home (house or garden); a public hall; and a club, hotel or restaurant. This gives rise to certain constraints on the means of provision, for a paid, non-family, caterer can provide a meal in any of these locations but the bride's mother cannot cook in a commercial environment. Delamont's scrutiny of suggested wedding menus suggests that there exists a fairly universal structure and content to such meals which, with drinks, runs from sherry, through salmon or lobster and wine, poultry and wine, a light pudding, wedding cake and champagne to coffee and tea. This suggested menu is harnessed firmly to the view that such a meal is a 'lunch' that is to follow a morning wedding. Similarly, many menus recommended predominantly cold dishes and a 'luxury' item such as salmon or lobster. These meals contrast to those offered by hotels which Delamont, drawing on her own research and that of others, found to be 'cooked dinner' type meals, characteristically comprising a soup, roast course with attendant vegetables, and a cold pudding (examples given include peach melba and sherry trifle). Two ideal types of meal are thus represented – one where the celebratory occasion is characterised by 'proper food' in strange surroundings (a hotel), the other where strange food is served in a familiar location (the home, a public hall).

According to Delamont, the significance of this patterning is to be found in the messages conveyed about 'proper' food and women's social role. In both types of reception, the bride is being dispatched into a new family unit and the wedding meal offers opportunities to the bride's family for the demonstration of skills and values which represent the kind of people they perceive themselves to be. Further, the reception illustrates to the groom and *his* family the kind of lifestyle to which the bride has been accustomed and thus what her expectations may reasonably be for the future. At the same time, each type of meal demonstrates the kinds of foods that the bride has been led to believe are proper and appropriate – and thus what her future husband may expect as part of his new wife's responsibilities. It is here that the 'message system' varies. The hotel-based 'proper dinner' reveals the family and bride's knowledge of what a 'proper' dinner looks like and reassures the groom of this fact while at the same time signalling that the bride is no longer entitled by right to have her dinners cooked for her by her mother: the public location of the wedding meal and the fact that it is catered by another, together with the financial costs involved, signal an end to parental indulgence in the form of personal service rendered to the daughter/bride. The home-based reception, in contrast, offers a different message, namely that the bride's mother is, according to Delamont:

> a cool, calm, collected hostess with organizing ability and technological resources . . . She saves money for her husband by catering herself, and displays that she is a better cook than the professionals . . . This reception shows . . . that the bride has been raised by, and hence will be, the perfect hostess, the highly organized wife. Only a family in good housing will contemplate a reception at home *from choice* so the financial standing of the bride's father is displayed by the setting of the reception . . . (Delamont, 1983: 149)

Delamont argues that class differences are reflected in each type of reception. The central position in the home of the work-ing-class woman is such that the reception on commercial premises makes the wedding non-normal because the working-class bride's mother does not cook and by not cooking, and taking a meal in the hotel/restaurant, reinforces the mundane nature of food preparation that is normally the woman's prime domestic responsibility. The middle-class home reception, in contrast, reflects the role of the middle-class woman as a manager of services which she purchases by virtue of her (husband's) affluence. The middle-class home is defined in terms of *external* influences on what is proper and appropriate. In performing the necessary services at the home reception, the bride's mother 'demonstrates that not only can she organise and cook, but that she can be seen to organise and to have cooked' (Delamont, 1983: 150) because of her appearance at the reception.

Though Delamont's findings may seem a little eccentric, they confirm among other things that at the heart of the menu system of hotels is the 'cooked dinner'. Indeed, cooked dinners occupy the same central position as a model of culinary provision in the hospitality industry as they do in the domestic food system. As Driver puts it, 'the interpenetration of home and restaurant cooking is now palpable' (1983: 178). However, it would be wrong to depict such interrelationships as a recent phenomenon. There is considerable historical evidence to suggest that the interpenetration of the private and public in catering in Britain and elsewhere can be traced at least as far back as the eighteenth and nineteenth century (Burnett, 1979). In more recent times, the *National Catering Inquiry* of the 1960s supported by Smethurst Foods produced a number of reports that reveal the extent of continuity between domestic and public food provision. The most important of these for the present purpose are *The British Eating Out* (National Catering Inquiry, 1966) and *Food Choice and Price: A Supplementary Report to The British Eating Out* (McKenzie, 1967).

In the first report, seven population centres were surveyed using questionnaire techniques, and the results provide an interesting insight into dining out in the 1960s. In terms of food choice, respondents were asked to select, on the basis of personal preferences, a number of courses from a list provided. The list comprised the most popular dishes served by restaurants at the time of the research (though how this was established is not explained), and caterers were asked to estimate customer preferences for the dishes on the list. The results of this exercise are summarised in Table 3.1. Some of the disparities between consumers' choices and caterers' beliefs about consumer preferences are striking and defy definitive explanation, though it is interesting to speculate that the quirk may be a methodological one, in that if the caterers asked were owners and managers, they might be less likely than their chefs and waiting staff to know what forms consumer demand take! The supplementary report published a year later (McKenzie, 1967) focused on a group of 420 people (half the sample from London, half from Leeds). Each respondent, eating out at least once a month, was asked to nominate one of three prices which most reflected their likely spending behaviour – five shillings (25 pence), twelve shillings and sixpence (62½ pence) and one pound – and were then presented with a menu within that price range and asked to choose a meal from it. For the most part, McKenzie concentrates on the twelve shillings and sixpence menu on the grounds that it matched most clearly the average price paid at that time for a meal (of thirteen shillings and two pence – around 66 pence in decimal coinage). In Table 3.2 however, the top three items for each course across all three price ranges are shown.

TABLE 3.1  Comparison of consumers' menu preferences and caterers' perceptions of consumers' preferences (per cent of those responding).

|  |  | Consumers | Caterers |
|---|---|---|---|
| Starters | Soup | 71 | 46 |
|  | Melon | 4 | 17 |
|  | Fruit juice | 3 | 14 |
| Main courses | Meat | 60 | 42 |
|  | Poultry | 10 | 26 |
|  | Mixed grill | 12 | 21 |
| Vegetables | Potatoes | 63 | 78 |
|  | Peas | 50 | 29 |
|  | Sprouts | 19 | 26 |
| Desserts* | Fruit salad | Pies/tarts |  |
|  | Pies/tarts | Ice cream |  |
|  | Cheese |  |  |
|  | Ice cream |  |  |

* Rankings only are given in source.
SOURCE:   National Catering Inquiry, 1966, pp. 13–17.

McKenzie's sample was small and the methodology uncertain, but two points can be made in passing. First, as the price range increases, then so, in the main, does the percentage of choices accounted for by the top three dishes diminish, suggesting perhaps (and assuming a class-income relationship) the greater flexibility of middle-class tastes. Second, and relatedly, within individual food categories there is some evidence – along the lines offered by Bourdieu (1984) in his observations on French domestic dining – that class-based tastes do exist. The preferences for soup, steak and kidney pudding, peas and steamed pudding on the five-shilling menu when compared to the prawn cocktail, fillet steak, sprouts and fresh fruit salad of the one-pound menu are suggestive.

TABLE 3.2   Restaurant menu choices by consumers at different prices (per cent response) (after McKenzie, 1967).

| | 5/- (25p) | | 12/6 (62½p) | £1.00 |
|---|---|---|---|---|
| *First course* | | | | |
| Soup | 76 | | 43 | 20 |
| Fruit juice | 19 | | 14 | 4 |
| Prawn/shrimp cocktail | N/A | | 24 | 25 |
| % of choices accounted for by top three selections | 95 | | 81 | 49 |
| *Main course* | | | | |
| Steak and kidney pudding | 24 | Fillet steak | 29 | 23 |
| Roast lamb | 17 | Roast beef | 11  Duck | 17 |
| Roast beef | 15 | Chicken | 10 | 14 |
| % of choices accounted for by top three selections | 56 | | 50 | 54 |
| *Potatoes* | | | | |
| Roast | 38 | | 35 | 21 |
| Mashed | 24 | | 19 | 15 |
| Sauté | N/A | | 14 | 21 |
| Chipped | 17 | | 14 | 21 |
| % of choices accounted for by top three selections | 79 | | 82 | 78 |
| *Other vegetables* | | | | |
| Brussels sprouts | 22 | | 29 | 21 |
| Peas | 29 | | 22 | 19 |
| Cauliflower | 17 | | 8 | 9 |
| % of choices accounted for by top three selections | 68 | | 59 | 49 |
| *Dessert* | | | | |
| Steamed pudding | 24 | Cheeses | 18  Fresh fruit salad | 28 |
| Fruit pie | 23 | | 18  Cheese | 21 |
| Tinned peaches/ fruit salad | 21 | Fresh fruit | 17  Melba peach/pear | 14 |
| % of choices accounted for by top three selections | 68 | | 53 | 63 |

By the 1980s, the range of public catering provision had expanded dramatically. Between 1983 and 1989, the trade magazine *Caterer and Hotelkeeper* carried an annual Gallup survey of trends in consumption. The popularity of dishes was again established by what caterers provided on their menus, so the survey results are necessarily a reflection of suppliers' perceptions of consumer tastes. For most of the period of the surveys, the cooked-dinner-type meal prevailed, often in the form of prawn cocktail, steak and chips and Black Forest gateau. In each survey, a great many sub-sectors of the industry were analysed, and variations in food choice between sectors were in evidence, though these were by no means radical. The 1989 survey was fairly typical of trends during this period (Wood, 1989). Covering twelve different sub-sectors of the hospitality industry including continental restaurants, burger joints, Chinese and Indian restaurants, and pizza operations, the 1989 survey did notice a minor change in trends – Black Forest gateau had suddenly become less popular! The typical lunch meal was soup of the day followed by fish and chips and then ice cream. For dinner, it was prawn cocktail, steak and chips and ice cream (Wood, 1989: 49). These findings contrast a little (but not much) with the results of a survey conducted by the Compass catering company in 1992. Compass (1992) examined working lunchtime habits in the twelve members of the (now) European Union. In the UK, the reported preferences of workers on their lunch break were, first, salad (twenty-nine per cent); second, fish and chips (eleven per cent); and finally steak and kidney pie and sandwiches in joint third place (ten per cent). Interestingly, steak figured in the top three choices of the French and Italians, and fried fish was also popular in France and Germany as well as the UK.

If the nature of, and demand for, public catering in these forms seems remarkably constant, then of equal interest is the extent to which gender and class relationships parallel (and occasionally diverge from) patterns of domestic dining, another theme hinted at in Delamont's analysis of the public-domestic interface of the wedding meal. One of the key issues to emerge from studies of domestic food preparation and consumption is that the 'cooked dinner' dietary system is primarily a male system that many women would not adhere to if they had a unilateral and unencumbered choice (Wood, 1992b). Masculine tastes also characterise the public provision of food in restaurants. Economic access is a crucial factor determining participation in public eating. The heavily segmented restaurant industry reflects this not only in its targeting of specific income groups but also in establishing key markets that outlets will serve: women shoppers, office workers, business executives and so on. Men and women generally have differential economic access to public catering facilities. Little research has been conducted into what implications this has for either female experiences of dining out, or for dining-out markets. Taken with the possibility that men and women have potentially differing values and tastes when it comes to food, the implications of these gendered differences within a predominantly 'masculine' restaurant industry are not inconsiderable. Unfortunately, in research terms there are only a number of informed assumptions and possible indicators of such influences at work. At the level of assumptions, within economic constraints there are reasonable grounds for believing that dining out offers some women some degrees of freedom to choose the foods they prefer when dining out. Two indicators of this (and probably other influences as well) are, first, the development by caterers of modes of food provision likely to appeal to women. Concessions to 'light' eating have become commonplace in restaurants of all types over the last decade or so, but caterers tend to construe 'lightness' in terms of diminished portion sizes of the dishes that they regularly serve, rather than the provision of different dishes. Second, here, women tend to be stereotyped by hospitality organisations' employees as fussy, demanding, low spenders, and poor tippers (Bowey, 1976; Mars and Nicod, 1984). This may well reflect to some extent a behavioural tendency on the part of female customers to seek to articulate their preferences more directly, though of course, as often as not, such behaviour is as much a reflection of women's economic disadvantage when dining out.

As consumers in restaurants and other public places, women are carefully controlled, or policed, and the stereotypes of female restaurant customers that abound in the hospitality industry are as much an aspect of the rhetoric of this control as they are a marketing judgement (Mazurkiewicz, 1983; see also Finkelstein, 1989 and Wood, 1994). Even in an industry where the majority of those engaged in food service are themselves

women, women as customers, as a market, tend to be marginalised and treated, in both abstract and concrete terms, as an
appendage to male clients or as part of a family unit. Women
customers are just as likely to attract opprobrium from female
staff for being fussy, or poor tippers, or making a coffee and a
cake last all afternoon, as they are from male staff. When a man
and woman dine together, it is still fairly common for the man
to be presented with the bill at the end of the meal, even if he is
not paying. Similarly, if beef and chicken are ordered, assumptions about gendered taste will often lead to the woman receiving the chicken, the man the beef. All these devices serve to
remind women that their presence is unusual and that they are
not strictly credible as consumers. In hospitality industry
employment too, similar stigmata are attached to female workers. The majority of waiting staff are women, and this rendering
of service in the public domain mirrors women's domestic role.
Interestingly, it is often assumed that most chefs are men.
Usually they are, but in the chef-cook occupational category
which tends to be used for statistical purposes by industry
bodies like the Hotel and Catering Training Company, around
a half of all chef-cooks are women (Wood, 1992a). The catch is,
of course, that most chefs are men while women tend to be
cooks, reflecting processes of occupational segregation characteristic of the patriarchal control over social relations.

Turning now to class, it appears that there is some merit in
Mennell's (1985) assertion that changes in dietary culture over
several centuries have led to 'increasing varieties'. Certainly,
there has been and continues to be substantial differentiation
(proliferation of varieties) in hospitality services according to
product (pizza/pasta; hamburgers; fish and chips; carveries for
'cooked dinners' and so forth) and marketers' concepts of
'brand'. Even stylised French cuisine has not escaped this
process, as is evidenced by the success of the Pierre Victoire
restaurants since their development in the early 1990s. However, it would be a mistake to believe that the processes of
product differentiation transcend class differences, thus 'diminishing contrasts' between classes. Careful segmentation of the
market by catering operators has been based as much on implicit
concepts of class markets as on the more 'people-friendly'
marketing categories, such as 'shoppers', 'office workers' and
business people. If market differentiation does not transcend

class differences, it is probably fair to Mennell to say that class differences often transcend market differentiation. Thus, many a middle-class parent will succumb to their children's pleas to visit McDonald's or Burger King. The role of children in family dining decisions is well-established in marketing research, but there is no evidence to suggest that adult preferences are anything more than (usually) at least partly class-based.

Tomlinson and Warde (1993) suggest fairly strong differences between four socio-economic occupational groupings: manual skilled and supervisory workers; intermediate white-collar workers; professionals; and industrial and commercial employers. Tomlinson and Warde's evidence suggests that manual and skilled and supervisory workers spend most of all the four groups on meals at work and relatively little on restaurants and street foods. Professionals spend heavily on restaurant meals but little on takeaway foods, while employers spend more on almost all foods outside the home (except food at work); at least twice as much on restaurant meals as intermediate white-collar workers, and almost twice as much as the manual working class; and, most interestingly of all, employers spend more heavily on takeaway and street food. This last observation would lend some credence to Mennell's democratisation thesis but for the fact that it appears (from the admittedly vague details supplied by Tomlinson and Warde) that the dining behaviour of this élite group is the behaviour of the generally privileged. As total spending on food outside the home increases, then so does the amount spent on all types of such food. General patterns of spending on food according to socio-economic position are not, however, the same as explicit preferences, though of course, in the absence of more extensive research findings, the issue remains an open one.

Less open to debate is Mennell's assertion that French haute cuisine has been in some way displaced from the apex of the hierarchy of food styles, a hierarchy that has been somewhat substantially levelled. Notwithstanding the occasional and fashionable interpolations into the hierarchy of culinary styles of such things as Japanese and Thai food, notable for example during the 1980s and still to some extent in vogue, French haute cuisine continues to enjoy dominance in the culinary hierarchy in many Western societies including Britain. To some extent it is true that connotations of 'Frenchness' and 'haute cuisine' have been diluted as a result of the increasing association of 'top' cuisine with individual chef practitioners. Chefs (or some chefs at least) are more than ever 'superstars', using their books, and access to television and radio, as vehicles for promoting their craft and themselves. The terms 'gastrosophy' and 'gastrosopher' have come to enjoy greater circulation, and designate those who both practise and appreciate the craft of cookery (Gillespie, 1993; 1994) as opposed to mere gastronomers who, with no practitioner skills, still set themselves up as arbiters of taste. According to Norman, some 800 books on food and drink were published in Britain in 1991 and, as she somewhat wearily notes, 'These days . . . expenditure is more likely to go on photography, design and production than on the text' (1992: 14). The resurgence of nouvelle cuisine (that is to say, its latest variant) during the 1970s and 1980s ensured that even where chefs were more important than their food, French styles of cooking remained pre-eminent.

More interesting yet in this context is Brunner's study of the training of British chefs. In a survey of eighteen colleges in London and the Home Counties, each offering catering education provision, Brunner (1985) uncovered a certain conservatism that goes some way to explaining the persistence of 'traditional' hotel and catering food. First, training provision was mainly oriented towards the commercial hotel and catering sector, and most catering apprentices, diplomates and graduates went into this sector (Brunner concedes that this might reflect regional bias in the survey, since some twenty-five per cent of all catering employment was, at the time, concentrated in the London region and there was evidence from elsewhere in the country that some colleges acted as 'feeders' for staff in the National Health Service; notwithstanding this, however, it seems to be normally the case that employment in the commercial hospitality industry is a generalised career goal among those involved in professional cookery, at least at the outset of their careers: see Chivers, 1973). Second, Brunner found few colleges making significant concessions towards healthier styles of cooking. Two colleges had run healthy-eating courses during the 1984–5 academic session, but more than half of the respondents persisted in the use of animal fats (for example, lard and dripping) and vegetable oils for frying. Tradition thus dies hard. This finding can be interpreted in another way, however, as seeking to produce foods cooked in a manner acceptable to a mass clientele. At the same time, avoidance of 'healthy cooking' reflects a more submerged ideological belief in British catering education that most hotel and catering consumers are interested, when dining out, in a predominantly hedonistic experience, and 'good food' correlates strongly in the minds of many with what is perceived as richer variants of domestic cuisine, produced using similar techniques. This is to some extent supported by Brunner's third main finding, namely that colleges persisted in emphasising the primary value of British and French cuisine in their teaching. None of the responding catering departments reported teaching West African, Caribbean or kosher cookery on craft courses, though seventy-five per cent did claim to teach elementary vegetarian main-course dishes and twenty-five per cent Asian, Oriental and wholefood cuisines. Twelve colleges taught predominantly British and French styles of cooking, with ten colleges also making special provision for the teaching of nouvelle styles of cuisine.

Thus, French cuisine – or at least imaginings of what French cuisine might be – still occupies its position at the apex of the British hierarchy of culinary styles, and, though not dominant in any quantitative sense, is still regarded as the epitome of gastronomic good taste. Like domestic dining, the public provision and consumption of food appears to be highly structured, and culinary structure continues to mirror and occasionally distort or rework social structure, the structure of social relationships between men and women and between classes. The continuities between domestic and non-domestic patterns of food consumption, the structures of this provision, and the social relationships bound up with provision, are striking and consistent. The earlier claim that, for the study of meals at least, 'structuralism works', has proved largely accurate. However, as indicated at the beginning of this chapter, the study of dining out provides a useful means of broadening theoretical analysis in the sociology of food and eating. To fulfil this manifesto, as it were, two concepts are of importance – standardisation and 'the meal experience'.

## STANDARDISATION: FROM CLASS TO MASS

While it is easy to be critical of some of Mennell's specific illustrations of 'diminishing contrasts' and 'increasing varieties', his model of change in British food habits retains a superficial appeal if only because it accords with certain common-sense beliefs about the march of progress towards a more democratic, more equal and less divided society. There is, however, another way in which diminishing contrasts and increasing varieties can be interpreted, not as the processual expression of democratisation, the proliferation of styles and greater civilisation of tastes in food habits, but as evidence of the standardisation and containment of food provision, processes that give only the illusion of democracy and choice.

This view, though more pessimistic than Mennell's, has much to commend it. Ritzer (1993), in his book *The McDonald-ization of Society*, offers a lucid restatement of Max Weber's (1864–1920) view of capitalist rationality as worked out in the organisational arrangements for the production of goods and services in modern industrial societies. In particular, Ritzer is concerned with Weber's concept of formal rationality, the extent to which 'the search by people for the optimum means to a given end is shaped by rules, regulations and larger social structures' (1993: 19). Formal rationality is a product of mainly modern, industrial societies, and the bureaucratic organisation is the 'paradigm case' of formal rationality. The growth of bureaucratic organisations is associated with certain ideologies that have shaped the nature of twentieth-century industrial production. In this respect, F. W. Taylor's development of 'scientific management', dedicated to the rationalisation of inefficient methods of industrial production through insistence upon ever more closely-defined specialisation and divisions of labour, is viewed as particularly important by Ritzer. In the realm of industrial production, bureaucratisation and scientific management, together with the assembly-line methods of working which they have encouraged, all add up to the process that Ritzer calls 'McDonaldization'. The terms is perhaps an unfortunate one: it is certainly unwieldy. Ritzer adopts it, however, to signal his assertion that the rationalisation traditionally associated with manufacturing industry has become just as much a key feature of services provision, including food service provision. This argument is not especially original, being a key theme of much post-1970s industrial sociology (see for example Braverman, 1974, whose influential arguments Ritzer clearly reflects). Interestingly, though, industrial sociologists (indeed,

sociologists in general) have for the most part completely ignored, marginalised or, at best, demonstrated transient interest in
service industries. To some extent, Ritzer's book is one of a
growing number of studies that go some way to rectifying
this neglect (see also the excellent but more specific parallel
study by Reiter, 1991). Ritzer takes fast-food restaurants as his
main case but extends the scope of his arguments to include
other services (for example, shopping malls, retail banking,
journalism, tourism services). He argues that rationalisation/
McDonaldization has four main characteristics.

The first of these is the emphasis on operational efficiency. In
fast-food restaurants and other highly rationalised organisations,
jobs and products are clearly defined, broken down into their
component parts and reintegrated in a manner that ensures
that the whole production process is conducted as quickly, efficiently and cost-effectively as possible. A limited number of
menu items makes obtaining supplies of raw ingredients a
more efficient process. Careful design of fast-food products
– the menu items themselves – means that, relative to available
technologies, food can be produced rapidly and to a uniform
cost and standard. These processes are all linked to models of
skill requirements such that employees can be taught quickly
and effectively to manage the food production system in a fashion that ensures efficient labour utilisation. Many rationalised
forms of service also entail putting the customer to work
through such means as self-service elements in the purchasing
process, thereby defraying the operator's costs by getting customers to perform tasks that would otherwise be undertaken
by employees. Examples of this include customers queuing for
their food, helping themselves to food (as with salad bars and
carveries) and disposing of their own debris once their meal is
completed. It is this putting the consumer to work that for
Ritzer indicates how what might be efficient for the operator is
not necessarily efficient for customers. As a product, the fast-
food meal is an apparently efficient way of satisfying the need
for food. It is quick and convenient, requiring none of the time
and labour involved in purchasing food from stores and
preparing a meal at home, nor involving the delays or costs
associated with a traditional restaurant meal. This superficially
consumer-friendly efficiency disguises, however, the work that
consumers often have to perform within the environs of the

fast-food restaurant. That many consumers do not perceive these elements as especially constraining is, in Ritzer's view, a testimony to the efficiency of fast-food restaurants' strategy of creating an image of fun for their operations so that they come to be perceived as places of public theatre and entertainment as well as places to eat.

The second major characteristic of McDonaldization is calculability. The rationalisation of production systems means that all aspects of the consumer service process are easy to calculate, from the time it should take for workers to serve customers to the cost of raw ingredients and their profit yield once processed. Ritzer suggests that while in many cases fast-food restaurants probably do offer more food for less money than conventional restaurants, the general image of value for money peddled to the consumer – of lots of food for little financial outlay – is often illusory. This is at least partly because consumers' expectations of the range and quality of food served in fast-food restaurants is not great, and their expectations of quantity are accordingly heightened. These expectations are met in a variety of ways, for example in the use of menu terminology that suggests size, in 'big' this and 'whopper' that, and by the use of carefully designed containers that, when filled, give the appearance of quantity when in reality the receptacles concerned give only an illusion of abundance.

McDonaldization's third main feature is its predictability. In the fast-food context, this includes the predictability of ingredients which both reassures customers as to what they are getting and encourages efficiency and calculability for the producer. Predictability is also inherent to fast-food products in that, from one outlet to the next, there is little variation in the range or quality of products. Indeed, this geographical homogeneity in standards is one of the selling points of fast-food products. That a particular product can look and taste the same in America or Europe is appreciated by many consumers who are reassured in knowing what they will get.

The final major element of the process of McDonaldization is control. In food production and food service, control (over quality, over production) is increasingly achieved by the use of technologies designed to minimise potential for human error while restricting the role of human labour to machine-minding. In fast-food restaurants, portion-control technologies are common in the form of the shape and size of receptacles into which food is placed, in the utensils used to serve foods, and in the machines used to dispense drinks. Control over customers is provided, according to Ritzer, by implicit techniques inherent to the conveyor-belt-like environments of fast-food restaurants, and by more explicit devices to ensure that customers purchase their food, eat it and leave, in as short a time as possible. One US chain seemingly plays 'Some Enchanted Evening' by Mantovani over its public address system in an effort to discourage teenagers from loitering outside its premises (Ritzer, 1993: 109). Sometimes, less subtle methods of control over customers are used such as the display of notices intimating limits on the time that customers can remain within the precincts of the restaurant.

The process of standardisation that Ritzer describes is one that in its modern form can be traced in origin to a specific epoch, the beginning of modern industrial production. It is, in this sense, a historical process. At the same time, standardisation is a contemporary process, an ongoing one, despite the whimsical protestations of writers who would seek to persuade us that we live in a postmodern, post-industrial world. More than this, standardisation is one of the vehicles by which some of the diminishing contrasts and increasing varieties in diet to which Mennell (1985) refers have been made possible. Capital investment in technology by food and food-related industries has, over the last 150 years, extinguished certain, previously unavoidable, contrasts in diet. The most obvious of these is, as Mennell notes, the seasonal availability of foodstuffs. Seasonality of foods matters now only insofar as people want it to matter. Ordinarily, a wide range of foodstuffs are routinely available all year round provided consumers do not mind them frozen, freeze-dried, canned or preserved in some other way. The technologies of food production, processing and storage, as well as those of transportation and distribution, have indeed diminished some contrasts.

However, this is not to say, as was intimated in Chapter 1, that one such contrast – the supposedly diminished distance between everyday and élite cuisine – has been narrowed in the sense stated by Mennell (1985). Indeed, processes of standardisation appear to have maintained class-related distinctions in food consumption. The main effect of standardisation has been to lower the barriers between domestic and public dining but only in the sense of expanding the market for particular types of food. Most people over the age of thirty can recall the introduction of pizzas and ready-made burgers (bun and all) into the range of products offered by supermarkets, just as earlier generations can remember the introduction of fish fingers and frozen chips. The interplay of economic and commercial factors has led to a situation whereby – if the pun can be forgiven – the hospitality, food-processing and food retail industries feed off each other. What is eaten in the home can to a very large extent be eaten in the restaurant. The interpenetration of domestic and public dining, both in terms of content and process, is generally recognised by Mennell (1985) who, however, sees the phenomenon as part of the playful democratisation of cuisine by which the lower orders have been exposed over time to increasing varieties of foodstuffs. To some degree this may be true, but the reduction of barriers between domestic and public dining is also as much a matter of containment of taste. Standardisation of provision, of supply, means that inevitably it is the markets of food suppliers rather than the choices afforded to food consumers that are expanded by reducing the barriers between domestic and public dining. As demonstrated earlier in the context of the hospitality industry, there is a broad match between what suppliers think consumers want and what consumers say they want, but there also exists a considerable dissonance and potential for dissonance in matching demand and supply. The power relationship between seller and buyer is biased in favour of the former. The ability of producers and suppliers to maintain existing markets and mould new ones is thus considerable and gives rise to two other important observations.

First, the whole process of standardisation is not confined to everyday cooking. The various forms of élite cookery are equally susceptible to standardisation and, in diluted form at least, are often readily accessible for domestic consumption via the local supermarket. In terms of this relative unity of domestic and public food markets, the very concepts of 'everyday' and 'élite' cookery are increasingly redundant. They remain important, however, precisely because it is in the interests of manufacturers and suppliers to maintain class-based distinctions in food preferences, thereby creating a larger market than would be the case if such distinctions did not exist. In other words, the persistence of class-based tastes is in the interests of food producers if people who eat burgers and pizzas in restaurants can be persuaded to eat them at home. As the president of McDonald's in the UK has put it 'Our menu is made up of meat, chicken, fish, salad. What we serve in McDonald's is nothing different from what you serve in your home' (Counsell, 1994). This lateral expansion of food markets across the domestic-public divide is an attractive option for suppliers because it diminishes any risks that might be incurred from trying to overcome the conservatism of food tastes through the introduction of new products outside of consumers' experience. It is also in the interests of suppliers to encourage stable and predictable markets, and hence stable and predictable demand for their products.

This is achieved, secondly, by encouraging perceptions of equivalency between different varieties of products within market segments. Thus in terms of 'everyday' food, a pizza is a burger is a spicy breadcrumbed chicken. All are broadly equivalent in the sense that they are close substitutes. Similarly, the élite haute cuisine or near-haute cuisine dishes that can be readily purchased from the supermarket come in many different varieties. Again, however, all are close substitutes. Paradoxically therefore, what makes for perceptions of equivalence within market segments are the apparent differences among the varieties of foodstuff on offer. Now, it may appear that the concept of close substitution is being used a little glibly here, and it is certainly necessary to consider what particular qualities might lend various apparently different products the status of close substitutes. The tentative response proposed is based on the observation that the true range of supplied food products which transcend the domestic-public divide is in reality very limited, yet perceptions of variety are sustained in the public mind. It is possible therefore that the qualities which lead to different foodstuffs being viewed as close substitutes are not intrinsic to the foodstuffs themselves. They are the qualities which, in Barthes's terms, transfer food 'into situation' such that 'situation' is more important than the food itself (Barthes, 1979; see Chapter 1, pp. 14–18). These include *inter alia* for any individual product: the convenience factors associated with the food product's preparation and consumption; control over when the product may be used (its preservation factor); the predictability of the product's quality; and the ease and efficiency with which the product can be stored.

The argument thus far, then, is that standardisation is one means by which both the interpenetration of domestic and public dining has been facilitated and continuities in domestic and public food provision established over time. An important aspect of these processes has been the creation of an illusion of variety, of choice, which has been achieved in part by the tendency of the food and hospitality industries to emphasise the value of the situational qualities of food rather than food itself. Variety and choice are believed to exist because relatively similar food products are perceived as possessing a range of secondary characteristics that, over time, consumers have been socialised into valuing more than any of the intrinsic qualities of foods. However, a choice of variant types of the same food product (for example, seven different kinds of pizza available in the local supermarket) or similar food products (pizzas, burgers, spicy breadcrumbed chicken) is not the same as a choice from a range of different foods, and may be no choice at all. The secondary characteristics that are used to sell foods encourage an underlying unity of modes of food provision at the level of food systems. What standardisation entails is a levelling of consumer expectations of food in both the public and private domain, a levelling of 'taste' in the only sensible sense in which that concept may be understood.

Of course, it may be fairly objected that these arguments apply only to a limited range of food products, namely those that form a common thread across the private-public dining divide. While conceding that this view has some legitimacy, it is also appropriate to note, following Ritzer (1993), that standardisation and rationalisation do not readily permit of innovation. The breakdown of the divide between private and public dining brings benefits to food suppliers by creating a free and expanded market for foodstuffs while at the same time stabilising an environment in which occasional, but not usually radical, innovation is possible. This can be seen to some degree in the extent to which products such as burgers – with their buns, salad, dressings and all – and pizzas conform (or have been made to conform) to the essential structure of the British meal or, more generally, to the carbohydrate-centrepiece-

dressing model of food consumption which has been shown to
have wide applications. Passariello makes a useful point in this
respect when she points to Mary Douglas's dictum that:

> a single dish will be considered a meal only if it
> incorporates the structure of the traditional meal in
> the particular culture in which it is served. Chicken
> Marengo (chicken fried with eggs and crayfish, in a
> tomato and garlic sauce) was a meal for Napoleon
> because it incorporated the structure of a traditional
> French meal: soup, fish, eggs and meat courses.
> (Passariello, 1990: 57–8)

Irrespective of whether individual food products come to be
considered a meal because of their structure, some rough paral-
leling of this structure is clearly essential if any food product is
to be successfully absorbed into a food system.

These issues can be further exemplified by reference to
Belasco's (1987) study of the rise of ethnic fast food in America
during the 1970s and 1980s. According to Belasco, the emer-
gence of ethnic fast foods in this period was a process 'wrought
by mass production' (1987: 2). That is, the growth of ethnic fast
foods was the result of corporate exploitation of a perceived
market opportunity, an opportunity that arose because of a
genuine growth of interest in ethnic foods. In terms of production, however, ethnic fast-food organisations moulded the
process in order to ensure that production was economic.
Methods of food presentation were also adapted in line with
prevailing American standards and preferences for fast-food
service. The range of ethnic fast foods produced as a result of
this engagement by capital with food were highly processed
and sanitised versions of the traditional dishes on which they
were modelled.

Taking a longer timescale than Belasco, Kraig (1988) charts
the incorporation of the hot dog into American cuisine from its
European origins. Kraig's central thesis is that the basic hot dog
is a kind of lowest common denominator, accessible to and
eaten by most Americans, irrespective of ethnic, class and other
differences. The standard hot dog is, however, subject to many
regional variations and these variations, in accompaniments,
and methods of preparation, reflect the prevailing mix of local
traditions and tastes which are the product of diverse historical

and biocultural influences. In other words, the content and presentation of the hot dog is adjusted to make it acceptable to local and regional dietary tastes. The process of adaptation is not a mechanistic one, though, at least not entirely. Rather, the many variations on the basic hot dog have evolved naturalistically over time. A similar process has been attributed to the absorption of non-indigenous cuisines into the British diet. Driver (1983) notes that British exposure to Chinese and Indian food has, historically, been closely related to trade and Empire. Prior to substantial immigration to Britain in the post-Second World War period, most Chinese and Indian food was known to the general population as just that, with there being little awareness of the internal diversity and differentiation of these cuisines. Further, most Chinese food provision in the restaurant sector was adjusted towards what were believed to be European tastes, namely 'lurid sweet and sour pork, inauthentic chop suey and chow mein' (Driver, 1983: 81). Immigration changed this to some degree, as many immigrants were from different areas and this was reflected in the diversity of culinary styles offered by those who went into the restaurant trade.

The general importance of these processes of adaptation and diffusion is widely recognised in the literature of the sociology of food and eating, though there are fewer detailed studies of them at work than might be expected given their importance. The work of Ritzer, Belasco, Kraig and Driver serves to emphasise the point that food adaptations can be contrived mechanistically through the attempts of the food industries to mould markets (the main vehicle of change and control here being the processes of rationalisation and standardisation), or can be the outcome of relatively organic processes of historical and biocultural change, of evolutionary social processes. Elements of both kinds of process may be evident in particular circumstances, as is witnessed by the effect of tourism on certain societies. Belisle (1983) examined tourism and food production in the Caribbean. Here, many of the potentially beneficial aspects of tourism are reduced by foreign exchange leakages, including the high import costs of foods and beverages for use in hotels. At the time of Belisle's research, food accounted for a third of tourist expenditure, and food imports had significant effects on the Caribbean economy. These included the loss of opportunities for local food production industries to expand, diversify and modernise and a corresponding loss of employment opportunities in the sector. In 1968, Jamaican hotels imported 69.4 per cent of their food supplies and 62.3 per cent of their beverages and cigarettes. In 1971, it was estimated that two-thirds of all foodstuffs eaten by tourists in Barbados were imported. There are many reasons that explain the buying behaviour of hotels and restaurants, the most important being that imported food is often cheaper than local food, and tourists are believed by hoteliers to prefer the type and taste of food they normally consume at home. Also significant, however, are the relationships that exist between foreign-owned hotels and overseas food suppliers. Taken together, these factors give some indication of how the beliefs and interests of business organisations can impact upon a food system. At the heart of Belisle's analysis is a sense of the extent to which fairly deliberate and contrived actions by suppliers can, over time, lead to what might broadly be termed organic change. The distortion of the Caribbean and other tourist economies in respect of food has taken time. What is less clear from studies like this is the extent to which Western food tastes impinge on the culinary culture of tourism hosts, though in the context of so-called Third World countries, the incomparable work of Susan George (1976) is suggestive of the potential for heavily marketed Western foods to distort indigenous cuisines and food consumption patterns.

Further clues as to the potential for such distortion in the tourism context are supplied by Reynolds (1993), who argues that 'If it is accepted that food is an indication of culture, then cultural change, as seen by the tourist, can be gauged by the availability of traditional dishes in local restaurants' (1993: 49–50). Reynolds studied twenty-eight restaurants in Sanus, Bali Island, all of varying market positions and all operated by owners or lessees. All the restaurants had examples of their menus going back five years or more. Analysis of these revealed that in 1988, fifty-two per cent of all dishes on the menus surveyed had their origins in Bali or Indonesia more widely. By 1992, this had fallen to sixteen per cent. Interviews with sixty-eight tourist patrons of the restaurants in the sample showed that fifty-eight per cent had expected a greater selection of indigenous dishes and seventy-two per cent were unimpressed by the attempts of restaurants to recreate Western dishes. The average number of dishes on a restaurant menu in

1992 was seventy-three, with a hard core of local dishes in each case. Reynolds notes that those restaurants offering a larger range of more traditional foods were at the cheaper end of the market, suggesting 'that the more "Western" oriented the operation, the more the flavours and textures of traditional dishes had been changed to suit Western palates' (1993: 52). The step-up in logic here is a little unclear, but the evidence of Belisle and Reynolds accords with knowledge of parallel processes of the adaptation of foods into alien environments. The point about Reynolds's analysis is that, again, it is unclear as to how Western foods had been incorporated, if at all, into the dietary consumption patterns of the host population. The willingness to cater for the perceived tastes of tourists, however, is indicative of a degree of voluntary change which may or may not come, in the future, to be recognised as one step in a process of the evolution of the host culture's diet.

## MEAL EXPERIENCES: THEATRES OF THE ABSURD?

There can be no student of hotel and catering management who has not heard of the concept of the 'meal experience' in one form or another, even if they have not read Campbell-Smith's original and influential text *The Marketing of the Meal Experience* (1967). From being an explicit concept, the 'meal experience' has now become a largely implicit one in catering and hospitality education and has wider currency among the dining public. At the time of the first publication of his book, Campbell-Smith's message was a fairly radical one. It was that when dining out, people are concerned not only with the nature and quality of the food they eat, but with the total environmental experience of dining out of which food is only a part. Campbell-Smith's book was the first serious quasi-academic articulation of this view and presaged the increased involvement of the professional marketing specialist in the higher reaches of the corporate hospitality industry.

Some twenty-two years later, Joanne Finkelstein (1989) was able to cast a sociologist's eye over the consequences of the application of this concept to the provision of public dining. Finkelstein's book, *Dining Out: A Sociology of Modern Manners*, was alluded to in Chapter 1. It is an important, if somewhat fluid contribution to theorising in the sociology of food and eating more generally because, as suggested earlier, Finkelstein attempts to steer a course through the structuralist-materialist-figurationalist minefield in order to forge a distinctive theoretical approach of her own. In this general respect, Finkelstein has much in common with Beardsworth and Keil (1990) though, unlike these authors, she is not interested in higher-level abstract theoretical models. Rather, Finkelstein adopts a highly pragmatic theoretical position but one that is heavily indebted to the work of Norbert Elias (1978). Unlike Mennell's (1985) application of Elias's conceptual framework, however, Finkelstein is concerned very largely with the present, noting Elias's view that as most changes in human behaviour tend to be unsystematic and defy accurate dating, it is of limited use to pursue the origins of such changes. Rather, Finkelstein somewhat eclectically plunders Elias's conceptual toolbox, at the same time drawing to some extent on the concepts of structuralist writers though, in both cases, explicit reference to the theoretical distinctiveness of structuralist and figurationalist approaches is largely lacking. To some degree this can, perhaps, be explained by the number of other theoretical perspectives and traditions that Finkelstein draws on, among them exchange theory and ethnomethodology. To the general reader, a detour into consideration of the nature of these concepts would be both tedious and of limited value for, as many professional sociologists would no doubt aver, Finkelstein's theoretical pragmatism can be seen more critically as theoretical dilution (cf. Beardsworth and Keil, 1990). This is not the view taken here. The preferred position is to argue that, warts and all, Finkelstein's position speaks very well for itself and with enviable clarity. Also, as will be shown in due course, the concept of the meal experience – and especially Finkelstein's perspective on it – is of considerable relevance to those arguments pursued by writers on the standardisation of foodways and food habits.

### *Uncivilised Sociality*

According to Finkelstein, contemporary dining out has much to do with self-presentation and 'the mediation of social relations through images of what is currently valued, accepted and fashionable' (1989: 3). Culturally, restaurants are regarded as places where excitement, pleasure and a sense of well-being will be experienced, and these and other images such as wealth and luxury are represented iconically within restaurants through such means as ambience, décor, furnishings, lighting and table-ware. So important are these iconic representations of people's emotional expectations, Finkelstein argues, that the 'physical appearance of the restaurant, its ambience and décor, are as important to the event of dining out as are the comestibles' (1989: 3).

Finkelstein's major theoretical position stems from a traditional philosophical concern of social scientists, namely an attempt to reconcile, conceptually, the individual with the social. The restaurant in society performs a double function, that of offering both an 'architecture of desire' and an inventory of the private, subjective world of the individual. In respect of the former, restaurants are places which constitute the loci of certain emotions which the restaurants themselves are instrumental in producing. Thus a sense of romance might be found in an exclusive and atmospheric bistro. Restaurants act as inventories of the individual's private world in that they allow people who visit them to demonstrate the value they attach to those activities and aesthetic forms that at any one time are regarded, culturally, as worthy of pleasurable response. In this sense, the individual who dines out is acting in something of an automatic way, realising desires that are effectively 'programmed' by society, reflecting prevailing cultural values as mediated by restaurants, and which are social rather than individual in character. This is, in fact, the essence of Finkelstein's argument. Individuals believe themselves to be acting from choice when they dine out, and they have expectations that restaurants will help them realise certain desires. These are not simply 'objective' desires – for good food and service – but expectations that restaurants will satisfy deeper emotional desires for status and belongingness. The fact that restaurants in all their varieties claim to be able to offer such satisfaction and indeed embody these desires is, however, indicative of how emotions have become commoditised. The social process whereby personal desires are supposed to be satisfied by various acts of public conduct is, for Finkelstein, a process of commoditisation, whereby emotions are transformed into commodities and 'sold' back to individuals as if they were consumer items.

This is heady and ambiguous stuff, but the direction of Finkelstein's argument is relatively clear. It is that, to a large degree, the desires of individuals are magnified and distorted by the marketplace. Some individuals have a desire for romance: some types of restaurant (claim that they) can satisfy elements of that desire, though there is no necessary or naturalistic cognitive association between romance and restaurants. Rather, as in the manner of structuralist analysis, such associations are semiotic in character. Thus, for a family 'meal', where the family comprises at least a young child or children, a restaurant such as McDonald's is an obvious choice, as the McDonald's chain embraces the concept of family fun and togetherness. The ambiguity of Finkelstein's argument lies in the extent to which concepts of the individual and individual choice appear to be relegated to the status of a cypher. There is a whiff of neo-Marxist determinism here in that individuals as consumers are represented as 'dupes', as merely dancing to the tune of consumer capitalism, not perhaps the most complex potential resolution of the conceptual tension between the individual and society.

Certainly, much of the rest of Finkelstein's analysis continues in similar vein. Dining out, she claims, is not an entirely individual act but one instance of the demonstration of 'uncivilised sociality'. By this, she means that restaurants are organisations which encourage certain styles of interaction that render dining out a mannered act. These styles of interaction are essentially imitative – of the behaviour of others, of prevailing images and fashions – and are actions of habit, without the need on the part of the consumer for thought, self-scrutiny or 'an examined life'. In other words, when dining out, Finkelstein argues, people behave within a framework of interaction already laid down for them, such that they for the most part withdraw from the social arena, from the need to engage meaningfully with others (Finkelstein, 1989: 5). Finkelstein's concept of uncivilised sociality is intended to convey this sense of disengagement of the individual from meaningful interaction with others. It occurs where individuals fail to examine the purposes of their actions, instead acting 'from habit or in response to the anonymous edicts of conventions' (1989: 12).

It is at this point in Finkelstein's argument that a very Douglas-like caveat is entered. Just as the latter claims that the boundaries of interaction associated with domestic food events (hot meals for family and intimates; cold meals for acquaintances;

drinks for casual associates and so on) are relevant only for so long as they have meaning for individuals, then so does Finkelstein argue that only if the individual accepts 'the fashions, regimentation and artifice of dining out as being legitimate and attractive features of the event' (1989: 12) does 'uncivilised sociality' as a form of behaviour stand as adequate description of consumers' responses to their circumstances. Once again, we see here a tension engendered by the intellectual struggle to accommodate meaningfully concepts of individual preference and choice within an essentially deterministic framework. This tension is complemented by another, namely the exact role played by food in the meal experience. As noted earlier, Finkelstein begins by attributing food an equal status in the meal-experience equation. Like the author of *The British Eating Out* report, obviously no sap to then prevailing fashions, Finkelstein appears to believe that 'In spite of the trend towards novel décor and a generally more "swinging" atmosphere, people still go to restaurants primarily for a good meal' (National Catering Inquiry, 1966: 12). As Finkelstein's argument progresses, however, the importance of food in her analysis diminishes and she suggests that status and costs are the most important differentiators of restaurant types because other factors, including the nature and quality of a restaurant's cuisine, are difficult to define objectively and therefore difficult to use as the basis for a classificatory scheme. This seems a somewhat curious argument since, in terms of the market position of a restaurant, higher status is usually associated with more rarefied forms of cuisine and such judgements are not normally confined to those accustomed to élite dining. A more interesting perspective on this aspect of Finkelstein's work is that within distinct market segments, some kinds of restaurant are regarded as higher in status than others. Thus, in the burger market, Chain A may be viewed as higher in status than Chain B, and chains in general may be better regarded than independents. This line of argument has much potential that is largely ignored by Finkelstein.

However, this is a small criticism of what remains a very persuasive argument, made more persuasive by the fact that Finkelstein does, eventually, to some extent reconcile the conceptual tension between the individual and society that lends her main thesis its deterministic qualities. She does this by introducing a rather subtle distinction between individuals as responsible for their actions and individuals not fully conscious of such responsibility (Finkelstein, 1989: 183), thus allowing that individual action of the part of consumers to avoid 'playing the game' represented by the challenge of uncivilised sociality is possible. She writes:

> Having asserted that individuals can rightly be thought of as responsible for their actions, it is necessary to point out that this is not the same as claiming they are fully conscious of that responsibility . . . For example, I know full well that I am responsible for choosing to dine in a bistro mondain rather than a local ethnic cafe. I have not been compelled or driven to do so, I simply choose to act in this way. However, if I am asked the question why I chose this restaurant and not that, and all I can offer as an answer is that I prefer the food here not there, or my companions suggested this one and not that, then I am only offering a personal idiosyncrasy as reason. I am not acknowledging any responsibility for the social status that dining out has as a source of personal pleasure, nor for the growing popularity of the practice, which of course would not occur unless I was willing to comply with the fashion . . . If the ability to articulate reasons for actions is a good basis from which to judge the development of an individual's consciousness, then it becomes reasonable to see inarticulateness in these matters as an equally good indication of the absence of full consciousness. (Finkelstein, 1989: 183)

### Standardisation and Meal Experiences

Finkelstein's arguments about uncivilised sociality are related (though not necessarily correlated) to those concerning standardisation. Standardisation is conventionally thought of as being production-oriented: products and the processes used to make products are standardised. The form of human labour inputs are, as far as possible, standardised, though human variability and intent makes the likely success of such processes more uncertain, as do attempts to standardise markets (that is, address or induce the expectations of particular audiences for specific products). Achieving the standardisation of markets, often considered difficult and unpredictable in business ideologies, may not be so complex to achieve if the arguments of writers like Ritzer (1993) and Finkelstein (1989) are to be believed. The message of the latter is that many consumers clearly subordinate themselves to the priorities of the restaurant – that is the values, mores and intentions of the restaurant. Emotions become commodities to be manipulated (or not) in much the same way as other elements in the standardised package of food provision that is the 'meal experience'. Moreover, consumers come to expect – relatively unconsciously – that these emotional elements to social exchange are legitimate aspects of the act of dining out, of consumption. Thus the standardised utterances of fast-food workers, conversational gambits and speeches scripted by corporate management, are an anticipated and expected element of that kind of experience, though 'Have a nice day' has yet to make the same impact in the cynical UK as it has done in the USA (see Kottak, 1978, for discussion of the manner in which the conversational styles of fast-food workers may be standardised through 'scripting'). Nevertheless, increasingly 'familiar' styles of food service are now fairly common, where waiting staff introduce themselves by name, hope their customers have a pleasant meal and regularly check to ensure that customers are indeed enjoying their experience. A more refined approach may well remain in élite establishments, but this is by no means sure, as overly attentive and solicitous waiting staff and precious chefs mingle with their clients in search of reassuring praise to shore up their fragile egos. One of the cheerfully mischievous aspects of an understanding of the process of standardisation is that it exposes the essential vulgarity of much of what passes for 'fine dining'.

Of course, *pace* Finkelstein, there are those who do not engage with the meal experience served up by restaurants, those who live an 'examined life'. By definition, however, such people constitute a minority. In terms of its employment practices and in some cases its production and marketing practices, commercial hospitality services is among the most exploitative of industries (Wood, 1992a). It would not be helpful to the success of the industry if consumers knew or thought this on every occasion they dined out. Similarly, the person who tells their friend who is complaining about the quality of food, or service, or ambience, that there are millions dying of starvation in the less developed countries is labelled a 'spoilsport' for shattering the fragile illusion of the meal experience. Food itself, and acts of dining out, have become so dissociated from the rhythms of life in the West that such comments are unwelcome intrusions into the reconstituted reality of the culture industries to which, increasingly, the public, commercial provision of hospitality belongs.

Nor, it must be said, is this reconstituted reality confined solely to the public domain. The term 'dining out' is misleading in at least two senses. First, nearly twenty per cent of meals served in the commercial hospitality sectors are in cafes and takeaways. While it is by no means easy to define the takeaway element, some two-thirds of fast food is consumed on a take-away basis (Wood, 1992b). This is, as it were, dining out to dine in, as many such food purchases are undoubtedly consumed in the home: standardised burgers, Indian and Chinese meals, and pizzas, all neatly packaged in boxes, mean that restaurant culture in at least one form is easily transferred back into the home – another mechanism whereby the interpenetration of public and private cuisine is facilitated. For the most part, with takeaways, the customer still provides the 'service' labour and the environment of consumption, but there is no reason to doubt seriously that the values attached, as it were, to the partial recreation of the restaurant in the home differ radically from those confronted when actually dining in a restaurant. An interesting sidelight on this is provided by analysis of the growing market for home deliveries of restaurant foodstuffs – long established in the USA but only more recently so in the UK. In respect of the fast-growing pizza home delivery market, Price (1993) observes that customers for these services are more likely to switch brands because of service quality (i.e. speed and effectiveness of delivery) than for price or product quality concerns, a case of non-food factors again being accorded greater importance than the food itself.

A second way in which the concept of dining out is misleading relates to the growing tendency for acts of public food consumption to be associated with, and secondary to, other activities (Cullen, 1985; 1994). Thus meals and drinks are combined in visits to local public houses, food is eaten on visits to shopping centres (the growth in number of the 'food courts' during the

1980s was phenomenal), leisure centres and cinema complexes. In short, dining out is no longer the singular activity it once was; it is not always an activity pursued for itself or in itself, but associated with other, mainly leisure, activities which are all part of a loose-knit collection of consumption-oriented services dedicated to making people enjoy themselves. The analogy with theatre and entertainment in general is unavoidable here and not wasted on writers like Finkelstein (1989) or many of the commentators on standardisation. In many cases, the elements of theatre in restaurants are an explicit part of the meal experience whereby waiting staff can and do juggle, bar staff know off by heart the recipes for hundreds of cocktails and can fulfil their orders in a variety of novel and skilful ways, and staff in general are encouraged to think of themselves as actors (Gardner and Wood, 1991). In these restaurants, the challenge is to be 'more theatrical than thou'. In the majority of cases, however, the effect is more subtle or at least less obviously theatrical, and it has thus become the case that the standardised meal experience, largely uncontemplated by those who participate in it, has entered the collective subconscious as a normal and indeed laudable aspect of eating out.

The arguments presented in this chapter offer a somewhat different and more varied picture to that articulated in much existing commentary on theory and research in the sociology of food and eating. It would, however, be impertinent to claim that the issues pursued here are evidence of anything more than the promised 'opening up' of existing debates and concerns in the sociological analysis of food and eating to other themes and issues. In the final chapter of this book, an effort will be made to draw together the various key elements so far considered in the text with a view to examining the status and potential utility of existing processes of theoretical modelling in the analysis of food-culture relationships.

# 4

# Conclusion:
## Theory, Meals and Society

The main theme of this book has been that a necessary corollary of the sociological study of the meal is an understanding of sociological theories pertaining to the development of food habits. In an area that remains a minority specialism within sociology, theoretical development evidences an apparent precocity that is arguably far in advance of empirical knowledge, with debates about theory reflecting entrenched and at times strongly-held views about the legitimacy or otherwise of what are invariably depicted as competing perspectives. One concern of the discussion so far has been to demonstrate that these perspectives should in fact be viewed as largely complementary. The overall approach of pragmatic structuralism adopted in this book is predicated on the view (so far noted on two previous occasions) that structuralism 'works', at least for the analysis of meals, providing a valuable framework for understanding the plethora of meanings that people bring to food use and consumption. For any writer in the field seeking that elusive academic quality of objectivity, reading the work of materialist, figurationalist and other developmentalist writers is suggestive of the need for the structuralist to offer embarrassed apologies for their predilections. The virulence of the former's views remains something of a mystery and on occasions seems out of all proportion to the issues under consideration. Then again, food is an emotional subject and it is possible to be somewhat sympathetic to those commentators who take exception to the clinical and at times admittedly reductionist approach of structural analysts.

Nevertheless, for the most part, a commitment to structural analysis needs no apology. The use of the term 'structural' is quite deliberate here in that, following Murcott (1988), it seems sensible to concede that pinning down any one theoretical approach that *is* structuralism is a futile task. At the same time, to adopt this term is not to retreat from the structuralist enterprise. The 'opening out' of the theoretical debate – if this does not appear too grand a description – presented in the previous chapter, notably in consideration of concepts of standardisation and uncivilised sociality, can be seen to lead to conclusions that are generally supportive of the viability of structural(ist) approaches. In this short concluding chapter, the intention is to expand upon this assertion by rehearsing the key arguments examined so far with a view to justifying the approach adopted, and pointing to its potential for further development.

## THE STRUCTURALIST CASE REVISITED

The main materialist criticism of structuralism is that it pays insufficient attention to biology and economics in explaining the origin and persistence of food habits. The main figurationalist objection to structuralism is that structural approaches are ahistorical and fail to explain both how food habits have come into being and the processes by which they change over time. The clearest criticisms of the materialist position's limitations, especially in respect of the work of Harris (1986; 1987) on food, are that empirical evidence is lacking or contradicts the materialist thesis (Fiddes, 1991), and materialists' assumptions about the rationality of consumer choice cannot be sustained (Douglas, 1984). Criticisms of the figurationalist view are less well established within the sociology of food and eating (but not within other areas of sociology – see Rojek, 1989), though several were intimated earlier in respect, specifically, of the work of Mennell (1985).

General limitations of the figurationalist approach can be discerned in the unproblematic status that writers like Elias and Mennell grant to historical method. In the case of food, it is argued that historical analysis is essential to an understanding of contemporary food habits and food consumption. However, both authors' treatment of primary historical sources could be argued to demonstrate more of a preoccupation with justifying rather than demonstrating the view that the civilising process is the motor of social change. In Mennell's case especially, there is a painful lack of awareness of contemporary issues in interpretative historiography (for a summary of some of these, see Jenkins, 1991), but Elias too has a tendency to accept his documentary resources at face value with little regard for the wider social contexts in which they were produced. The scholarship of both writers cannot disguise the fact that there is no single unifying concept that is 'history', and that the constitution of historical accounts is necessarily a social process that reflects the interests and enthusiasms of those who produce them.

One analysis that goes some way to combining the general theoretical orientations of both materialists and figurationalists is that offered by Harris and Ross (1978), who chart the transition of the dietary system in the USA from its dominance by pork to dominance by beef. Harris and Ross argue that beef-eating in the USA is a recent and probably temporary phenomenon that has grown out of technological changes engendered by the attempt to maximise benefits and minimise the costs of meat production in the face of shifting ecological and demographic considerations. Historically, prior to about 1875, pork was the preferred daily meat of Americans and was marginally the most popular as late as 1950. The pre-eminence of pork was due to the biological efficiency of the pig in converting plants into flesh, the fact that pigs were easier than other livestock to care for, and that they possess a tendency to have large litters. Also, an excess of corn relative to human needs was at first converted into Bourbon whisky until federal taxation meant that farmers found it more profitable to convert such corn into pig feed. By 1830, the 'hog belt' had reached Cincinnati (Porkopolis), and it subsequently moved further west, with Chicago replacing Cincinnati as the 'hog butcher to the world'. Up until 1860, cattle had two disadvantages as a source of mass-produced meat – pork was cheaper, and its preservation was more safely assured through salting. However, after this date, the growth of beef production began. Large areas of the USA beyond the Mississippi and in the western rangelands were arid and semi-arid grasslands, unsuitable to corn production. Cattle were thus more efficient as a source of investment than pigs. Cattle are good digesters of grass, pigs are not, and cattle could thus more efficiently convert plants into meat. Until this time, cattle were largely favoured for their hides. The growth of the railways opened up valuable eastern markets for beef as food. Further, in order to reach urban markets, cattle could be driven and made to cross rivers, difficult feats for pigs. Penetration of the eastern markets of the USA was further assisted by the growth of refrigerated transport. Beef's reputation was, according to Harris and Ross, thus established on the basis of practical production and marketing breakthroughs that made fresh beef available to the urban consumer.

This account combines elements of the materialist and historical approaches to an understanding of the origins of food habits in a persuasive manner, with historical evidence put to good use in illuminating the role of biological, geographical, political, economic and industrial factors in influencing the development of foodways. Yet these 'commodity histories' tell us little about the ways in which macro-social changes in diet influence the micro-social world – the everyday means attached to foods and the uses to which foods are put. A strict figurationalist would undoubtedly elaborate Harris and Ross's analysis to examine the cultural factors that encouraged the assimilation of beef into the dietary system. It is doubtful that the essential determinism of either approach could be entirely obscured, however. Despite protestations to the contrary, both materialist and figurationalist approaches to food and eating rely crucially on a linear view of the evolution of food habits in which the behaviour of consumers 'feeds back' into the evolutionary process only as a response to 'objective' imperatives, whether these be biology or the civilising process. Individuals and groups are regarded as essentially reactive in the systems of consumption envisaged by materialists and figurationalists, rather than as being actively engaged in the day-to-day elaboration of dietary culture and meaning. In this light, the claims of materialist and figurationalist writers to analytic dynamism appear somewhat empty. In contrast, structuralist approaches appear far from static, concerned as they are with the fluidity of meaning that people bring to acts of food consumption. The argument that structuralist analysis seeks stasis beneath the flow of human social behaviour has never been very persuasive, though it is perhaps fair to say that the many varieties of structuralism are preoccupied with (in a once fashionable socio-logical phrase) 'the ethnocentricity of now'.

However, this is a far cry from arguing that structuralists seek explanations of social phenomena to establish definitive patterns of social behaviour. Indeed, in the arena of the sociology of food and eating, it can be argued with some conviction that the limitations of structuralist analysis derive from an excessive conceptual fluidity. Goody's (1982) assertion that many struc-turalists appear to 'decode' the 'language' of cuisine differently has some force here, a considerable irony given Goody's equally emphatic assertion that structuralists seek definitive models of social relationships (see Chapter 1). Nowhere is the conceptual fluidity of structuralism more evident than in studies of the meal, where the breathless proliferation of hard-nosed empiri-cal studies of meal-taking has had scant regard for conceptual continuity and coherence. In depicting the many ways in which meal structures are 'filled' as variations on a single theme, structuralist writers too easily and too often rely on assump-tions about the inviolability of the core concepts which they employ. Instances of the diversity with which meal structures are filled may as much indicate the inability of these concepts to cope with such diversity as suggest some abstract 'theme with variations'. Two examples will serve here to illustrate this point.

First, there is structuralists' attachment to the concept of the essentially shared nature of food consumption in the form of the meal. All the studies reviewed earlier, however, suggest that meals are only part of the domestic food system, and some evidence indicates that there are occasions when meals are taken alone, in isolation from others. It is not acceptable to argue, therefore, that the presence or absence of others is a defining feature either of the meal experience or of food con-sumption in general. Structuralists' preoccupation with the social qualities of the meal leads to consideration of only part of people's everyday culinary experience, the concept of the meal being granted a privileged analytic position, and 'non-meals' being relegated to the periphery of analysis.

A second instance of how the fluidity of structuralist analy-ses of meals presents conceptual problems lies in the extent to which exceptions can or cannot be incorporated within an overall analytic framework. Studies of the meal in the British and US social anthropological and sociological traditions are, for example, ill-equipped to cope with concepts of 'family service' where multiple dishes are made available for one or more courses in a meal, as in the case of the working-class families described by Bourdieu (1984). Further, as Hazan notes in the Italian context:

> There is no main course to an Italian meal. With some very rare exceptions such as *ossobuco* with *risotto*, the concept of a single dominant course is entirely foreign to the Italian way of eating. There are, at a minimum, two principal courses, which are never, never brought to the table at the same time. (Hazan, 1981, quoted in Mars, 1983: 145)

Hazan's comments could apply equally to the analysis of Japanese meals as indicated in the earlier summary of Befu's (1974) work and could no doubt have more general relevance for different societies. In this sense, the concept of structure cannot be generalised uncritically. However, it would be a mistake to argue that, in principle, models of meal structure must necessarily be culture-bound. The conceptual flexibility of structuralism should permit of the construction of comparative models – should, in other words, seek some of the coherence and stasis that structuralism's critics see as inimical to the approach but which in practice is hard to discern beyond structuralists' attempts to provide descriptions of social reality in much the same manner as their would-be theoretical competitors.

That, for the most part, the extension of structuralist analysis in this manner has not taken place is largely a result of the micro-sociological methods adopted by most analysts of the meal, methods which rely too much on a case-study approach and an exaggerated commitment to the subjectivity of social actors' own perceptual categories, a shying-away from the possibility that the perceptions that social actors bring to acts of food consumption can be systematically ordered for the purposes of comparative analysis. In this sense, structuralist analysis amounts to little more than the practice of particular analytic methods and the description of related elements with culinary systems. The corollary of this view is that where structuralist analysis has been more ambitious in attempting some fusion between macro- and micro-social approaches to the study of food and eating, higher-order comparative explanations of social behaviour have been forthcoming, most notably in the work of Bourdieu (1984) where, however, the comparative dimension involved examination of related cultural forms in a single society.

The significance of Bourdieu's work lies, of course, in the manner in which a large array of influences are examined in an effort to paint a bigger explanatory picture. Without becoming involved in deeper philosophical debates about the nature of what constitutes 'explanation', Bourdieu's work does offer a highly convincing account of, *inter alia*, the formation and role of food-related behaviours and one, moreover, that eschews both the abstract determinism of theoretical perspectives complementary to structuralism (and indeed more abstract and generalised structuralist accounts of the kind advanced by Barthes, 1973) and the limiting and introspective case-study approach to the study of meal structures. Having said this, it is important not to exaggerate the limitations of the case-study approach. The explanatory power of this method is testified to more than adequately by the consistency of the findings of different studies in respect of the role of meal-taking and food consumption in family and domestic contexts. That it is quite possible to extend usefully the concepts and techniques employed in such studies to the arena of public dining and to higher levels of explanatory generalisation was demonstrated in Chapter 3. The single key reservation about the case-study approach is that its many practitioners have not seized the opportunity to synthesise the related but usually distinct conceptual frameworks that they employ. This absence of simple construction work, of any serious attempt to integrate existing, individual research approaches, is what lends the body of work on meal analysis its 'piecemeal' character – in both appearance and substance – and has so far inhibited the development of an intellectual common ground capable of forming the basis for meaningful comparative studies of meal structures and food systems in different social and cultural contexts.

Despite these reservations, it can be argued with some confidence that far from being 'on the ropes', structuralist analysis of food, eating and the meal is alive and kicking. A pragmatic structuralist approach to the study of food habits still offers the best means of uncovering the tapestry of meanings that people weave around food consumption. For all their sombre authority, materialist and figurational approaches are informed by largely abstract assumptions that are difficult to exemplify empirically and which limit their explanatory power to highly generalised accounts of human behaviour which stop short of the detailed examination of social action and interaction. More importantly perhaps – and certainly as far as figurationalism is concerned – both perspectives are guilty of the tendencies which they readily attribute to structuralists and structuralism, namely a preoccupation with forces that underpin and determine social behaviour ('biological imperatives', the 'civilising process'). The theoretical and methodological criticisms of materialist and figurationalist approaches need not be reiterated, save to say that any theoretically *a priori* approach is, ultimately, bound to be limited in how it can be operationalised for the purposes of practical research.

## STRUCTURALISM, THEORY AND MEALS

In examining in this work the ways in which sociologists and other social scientists have approached the study of meals and meal-taking in society, emphasis has been placed on the centrality of the meal in sociological analyses of food and eating. It is not simply the case that the study of meals has formed a substantial part of research within the sociology of food, though this is true, but that acts of food consumption routinely take the form of what we know and term as meals.

The discussion in the preceding section alluded to possible dangers associated with granting meals, as acts of food consumption, a privileged analytic status. Despite these caveats, it is difficult to avoid the conclusion that, contrary to the occasional siren voices raised in opposition, meals remain at the heart of British and other culinary cultures, constituting perhaps both the ideal act of food consumption as well as epitomising more generally systems of food consumption. Moreover, in theoretical terms, in terms of the systematic exploration of the cultural significance of food in society, the more that researchers distance themselves from the micro-social aspects of food consumption, the greater is the danger that explanations of food-related behaviour will be pitched at levels of such abstraction and generalisation that the depth and detail of this behaviour will be obscured. The more profound theoretical issues apart, it is this observation more than any other that suggests the need for caution in the treatment of materialist, figurationalist and other 'developmental' perspectives on the sociology of food and eating.

At the same time, these approaches cannot be ignored for, as demonstrated at various points in the text, they raise conceptual issues of some importance to an understanding of food-culture relationships. Advocating a view of theoretical perspectives other than structuralism as complementary to the latter in the analysis of food-culture relationships is not just a matter of rhetoric, however, but a necessary methodological strategy in the light of the limitations of these approaches. The sad paradox of materialist, figurational and other developmental approaches is that their professed theoretical dynamism leads them ultimately to a view of food habits and consumption as to a large extent fixed by factors exogenous to the actions of individuals, where the meanings of acts of food consumption are reduced to the status of 'dependent variables', dependent on *a priori* constructs of the order of biological imperatives or civilising processes.

This view is, of course, at the heart of Beardsworth and Keil's (1990) thoughtful critique of the state of theorising in the sociology of food and eating. Their alternative theoretical model is itself highly pragmatic in nature, advocating the integration of process and structure in analyses of food-culture habits. In this context, it appears that 'process' refers both to historical processes and the processes of production and consumption that might broadly be viewed as constituting the food chain – hence biological factors are also included within the proposed framework. It is not easy to envisage what, in practice, actual studies couched in these terms would look like. The earlier noted work of Harris and Ross (1978) on the role of pork and beef in the US dietary system would perhaps represent a proto-typical example of the kind of approach that Beardsworth and Keil have in mind, following, through history, the economic, ecological, biological, production and technological influences on food production and then, unlike Harris and Ross, perhaps extending the research process to consider the symbolic and aesthetic aspects of consumption that in turn influence the other elements in the cycle of production and consumption. It is difficult in principle to raise any serious objections to the research strategy suggested by Beardsworth and Keil, a combination of both macro- and micro-social perspectives and methods of study combined in pursuit of holistic explanations of food consumption. In practice, however, the underlying tone of this approach is more than a little utopian and idealistic, if only in its expectation that academic researchers could unite around this single agenda! Of greater concern is the extent to which the pragmatism inherent in Beardsworth and Keil's approach may, in explanatory terms, tend towards the descriptive as a result of the absence of any unifying theoretical framework within which to assess the relative importance of different influences on the formation and maintenance of food habits. Also, at the level of research practice, the sheer enormity of the framework proposed by Beardsworth and Keil raises doubts as to whether any programme of investigation could be adequately operationalised. In consequence, it is probably best to regard their approach as a long-term aspiration, an ultimately realisable theoretical state of grace towards which researchers should work.

In the medium term, however, sociological analysis of food and eating might better proceed by pursuing, in the language of the American sociologist Robert K. Merton (1949), 'theories of the middle range', that is theories that lie somewhere between the disparate micro-sociological concepts, hypotheses and theoretical conjectures of single research projects and the grand theoretical schemata that seek to provide all-encompassing explanations of social phenomena. In terms of Merton's categories, structuralism itself is difficult to place: on the one hand it possesses in some forms many of the characteristics of grand theory; on the other it can be preoccupied with the micro-social aspects of behaviour to the extent of appearing, on occasions, obsessed with the trivial. If we regard these categories as more of an exhortation to consider the value of a particular style or method of approaching social analysis, then, in the context of the structuralist investigation of food consumption, Bourdieu's (1984) work must stand as one of the most persuasive 'middle-range' theoretical studies of food-culture relationships to date, linking as it does examination of food consumption at the level of both the individual and the group to wider social trends and patterns.

Sociologists (including structuralists) committed to uncompromisingly interpretative approaches to the study of cultural phenomena may scoff at the raw empiricism that underpins the style of research favoured by Bourdieu, but there can be little doubt that, even allowing for disagreements over the interpretation of data, this kind of research strategy permits of a modest level of explanatory generalisation without neglecting entirely the micro-social aspects of human behaviour. Of course, Bourdieu's analysis at this level lacks detail and in places is highly impressionistic, but this in no way diminishes his overall achievement in establishing linkages between such behaviour and wider aspects of social structure. More important is the extent to which Bourdieu achieves a balance in perspective, treating the meal as central to, but not dominant in the overall analysis of food consumption patterns.

All this is achieved by the 'opening up' of the study of food consumption to examination of the role of wider social factors in the constitution of meaning, and in particular the role of class. In this respect, it is possible to argue after Beardsworth and Keil (1990) that Bourdieu treats food simply as a 'dependent variable'. Yet Bourdieu avoids postulating simplistic causal links between class and food consumption in, for example, his description of how a working-class pattern of food consumption characterised by 'congenital coarseness' persists even in circumstances where increased economic power could facilitate an adjustment of diet and to levels of refinement in line with middle-class conventions.

Bourdieu's work, then, offers one possible model for future investigations informed by broadly structuralist concerns, combining as it does both theoretical sophistication and a pragmatism that guards against excessive preoccupation with the insular, micro-social methodologies of the case-study approach and the abstract generalisations of those who advocate a less empirically anchored approach to the explanation of food-related behaviour. Two caveats may be entered at this point. The first is that while the broadening of analysis is essential to ensuring a sense of perspective, it would be unfortunate if the potential of conceptual synthesis were lost in respect of the comparative analysis of meal structure. Second, accounts and explanations of social behaviour in terms of class can be regarded with some validity as normally embracing a fairly high level of generalisation, and Bourdieu demonstrates this in his tendency, on occasions, to make fairly sweeping assertions about the relationships between class and food consumption. This suggests perhaps that, in opening up the micro-social analysis of food, eating and the meal, it may be necessary to select even more modest themes on which to concentrate in developing a meaningful research agenda.

In Chapter 3, one such theme was considered in broad terms, namely standardisation. The process of standardisation is relevant to an appreciation of how food consumption has, in qualitative terms, changed and been changed over time, and is of particular value to assisting understanding of the place of meals within the dietary system. At the same time, the concept of standardisation has much wider applications within social analysis, capturing as it does the essence of long-term trends in production and consumption. Uncivilised sociality, with its more specific origins in Finkelstein's (1989) re-reading of Elias (1978), cannot be treated in quite the same way, as it is a concept more difficult to demonstrate empirically. However, it is a concept with some potential in the context of other accounts that have identified, *contra* Elias, counter-tendencies to the civilising process in the form of 'un-civilising' processes that act against the long march of civility envisaged by figurationalists (see Rojek, 1989).

In academic circles, it is generally regarded as bad form to introduce new ideas in the conclusion to a work. Nevertheless, there is some pleasure to be gained from adopting the 'light the blue touchpaper and retire' principle, and it would be wrong to neglect the potential importance of one other set of themes relevant to an understanding of food consumption – namely those associated with marketing. The importance of food marketing is recognised by writers as diverse as Barthes (1973) and Mennell (1985) but elsewhere has been neglected. As the earlier discussion on standardisation suggested, however, individuals and groups of consumers are not alone in imbuing food products with particular meanings, and the study of the interplay of these meanings and their degree of acceptance and rejection within cultures and societies may reveal much about the success or otherwise of the marketing communications practices of the food industries as they seek to influence the culture of food consumption (Gofton, 1989).

These then are just some suggestions for themes around which the kind of pragmatic structuralist analysis of food, eating and meals advanced in this book might be organised. There are, no doubt, others. The case for a more developed structuralist analysis in the sociology of food and eating is a strong one. The structuralist approach is, for the time being at least, the only perspective that can adequately reflect the central reality of acts of food consumption (that, whether one likes it or not, people actively structure such acts in a manner which reflects their perceptions of reality). Perhaps more significantly, the theoretical case against structuralist analysis has not been made – or has certainly been found wanting. In this respect at least, there is a sense in which structuralist approaches are the best of a bad or limited lot, for they do have serious limitations. An honest effort has been made to expose some of these in this text, while at the same time suggesting in broad terms how they may be ameliorated in future research. There are few statements which summarise the variety of influences with which the sociologist of food and eating must contend with more elegance than Gofton's remarks to the effect that:

> Food consumption practices are social constructs; the system which they form cannot be understood apart from the ways in which it interrelates with other social institutions, in the process of historical development. At one and the same time, the system provides a communicative resource, a language, which both expresses the main themes and values of the society and enables individuals to pursue their individual projects and purposes. Every occasion of usage is, then, both a reaffirmation of a world view and a subtle modification of its shape as the individual interprets and restates it. (Gofton, 1986: 131)

### CLOSING REMARKS

As indicated at the commencement of the previous section, the meal is alive and well in British and other cultures. It also retains its importance as the phenomenon at the heart of the social scientific analysis of food and eating, a point which this book has sought to illustrate in terms of both the strengths and limitations of particular theoretical and empirical approaches to the study of the role of the meal in society, and the implications of meal-taking for food consumption more generally. In writing this book, an effort has been made to combine simple reportage with a particular point of view that arises from engagement with existing debates in what often appears to be an overly complex area of social investigation marked by premature theoretical moribundity. Any academic author who seeks such engagement and challenges, however modestly, existing orthodoxies in a particular field opens himself or herself up to critical reprisals. This is so much the better: the sociology of food and eating as a distinctive area of social inquiry has attracted little sustained attention. Despite the generally high quality of contributions to the area thus far, there is at present little evidence of meaningful progress in the field and more than a whiff of theoretical entrenchment, even complacency, in recent commentaries on the 'state of the art'.

It is sad, but by no means difficult, to accept that modern sociology, with its predilections for navel-contemplation and obsessions with intra-disciplinary debates, has managed largely to ignore both that phenomenon (food) and activity (eating) which are absolutely fundamental to human existence. It is tempting to observe that food is, in any case, too important a topic to be left to sociologists alone! Certainly, a multi-disciplinary approach to the topic is, for reasons outlined in Chapter 1, not only desirable but largely unavoidable. Having said this, there is some hint of a suggestion that if sociology was ever, for a time, the focus of dynamism in research into food-culture relationships, this focus may now be shifting, as is evidenced by the quality of work being produced by historians (e.g. Visser, 1986; 1992) and philosophers and psychologists (Curtin and Heldke, 1992), which appears refreshing and challenging where sociological debates seem turbid and dull.

It would be presumptuous to suggest that the sociological analysis of food and eating needs to be rescued from itself, but there is a case for arguing that if its potential is to be fully realised, sociological analysis needs to build consistently on its early foundations rather than descend into dubious arguments about whether the foundations should be changed and replaced. In this way, the scope of sociological inquiry might be broadened beyond both the essential circularity of current theoretical debates and the limitations of existing empirical research.

Whatever form future research takes, however, there can be little doubt that the meal will retain its central importance as the principal model on which routine acts of food consumption are based.

# References

Allen, D. E. (1968), *British Tastes*, London: Panther.

Barthes, R. (1967) [1964], *Elements of Semiology*, London: Jonathan Cape

———— (1973) [1957], *Mythologies*, London: Paladin.

———— (1979) [1961], 'Towards a psychosociology of contemporary food consumption', in R. Forster and O. Ranum (eds), *Food and Drink in History*, Baltimore: Johns Hopkins University Press, pp. 166–73.

Batstone, E. (1983), 'The hierarchy of maintenance and the maintenance of hierarchy: notes on food and industry', in Murcott, A. (ed.), *The Sociology of Food and Eating*, Farnborough: Gower, pp. 45–53.

Beardsworth, A. (1990), 'Trans-science and moral panics: understanding food scares', *British Food Journal*, 92, 5, pp. 11–16.

Beardsworth, A. and Keil, T. (1990), 'Putting the menu on the agenda', *Sociology*, 24, 1, pp. 139–51.

———— (1991a), 'Vegetarianism, veganism and meat avoidance: recent trends and findings', *British Food Journal*, 93, 4, pp. 19–24.

———— (1991b), 'Health-related beliefs and dietary practices among vegetarians and vegans: a qualitative study', *Health Education Journal*, 50, 1, pp. 38–42.

Befu, H. (1974), 'An ethnography of dinner entertainment in Japan', *Arctic Anthropology*, 11 (Supplement), pp. 196–203.

Belasco, W. J. (1987), 'Ethnic fast foods: the corporate melting pot', *Food and Foodways*, 2, 1, pp.1–30.

Belisle, F. J. (1983), 'Tourism and food production in the Caribbean', *Annals of Tourism Research*, 10, 4, pp. 497–513.

Bennett, J. W., Smith, H. L. and Passin, H. (1942), 'Food and culture in

Southern Illinois – a preliminary report', *American Sociological Review*, 8, 5, pp. 561–9.

Bottomore, T. and Nisbet, R. (1979), 'Structuralism', in Bottomore and Nisbet (eds), *A History of Sociological Analysis*, New York: Basic Books, pp. 557–98.

Bourdieu, P. (1984) [1979], *Distinction: A Social Critique of the Judgement of Taste*, London: Routledge and Kegan Paul.

Bowey, A. M. (1976), *The Sociology of Organizations*, London: Hodder and Stoughton.

Braverman, H. (1974), *Labor and Monopoly Capital*, New York: Monthly Review Press.

Brunner, E. (1985), *Catering for All? A Survey Report on Catering Education in the London Area, 1985*, London: London Food Commission.

Burnett, J. (1979), *Plenty and Want: A Social History of Diet in England from 1815 to the Present Day*, London: Scolar Press.

Campbell-Smith, G. (1967), *The Marketing of the Meal Experience*, Guildford: Surrey University Press.

Carmouche, R. (1980), 'Social class in hotels', mimeograph, Department of Catering Studies, Huddersfield Polytechnic.

Charles, N. and Kerr, M. (1988), *Women, Food and Families*, Manchester: Manchester University Press.

Charsley, S. R. (1992), *Wedding Cakes and Cultural History*, London: Routledge.

Chivers, T. S. (1973), 'The proletarianisation of a service worker', *Sociological Review*, 21, pp. 633–56.

Clark, J. and Platt, J. (1984), 'The pack a punch lunch', *Nutrition and Food Science*, 91, 14–15.

Coleridge, N. (1993), 'Whatever happened to Sunday lunch?', *The Sunday Telegraph*, Review, 28 March, p. 1.

Compass (1992), *The European Lunchtime Report*, London: Compass.

Counsell, G. (1994), 'The big boss eats his own words', *The Independent*, 3 April, p. 18.

Coxon, T. (1983), 'Men in the kitchen: notes from a cookery class', in Murcott, A. (ed.), *The Sociology of Food and Eating*, Farnborough: Gower, pp. 172–7.

Cullen, P. (1985), 'Economic aspects of hotel and catering industry changes', *International Journal of Hospitality Management*, 4, 4, pp. 167–71.

——— (1994), 'Time, tastes and technology: the economic evolution of eating out', *British Food Journal*, in press.

Culler, J. (1983), *Barthes*, Glasgow: Fontana.

Curtin, D. W. and Heldke, L. M. (eds) (1992), *Cooking, Eating, Thinking: Transformative Philosophies of Food*, Indiana: Indiana University Press.

Dare, S. E. (1988), 'Too many cooks? Food acceptability and women's work in the informal economy', in Thomson, D. H. (ed.), *Food Acceptability*, London: Elsevier, pp. 143–53.

Delamont, S. (1983), 'Lobster, chicken, cake and tears: deciphering wedding meals', in Murcott, A. (ed.), *The Sociology of Food and Eating*, Farnborough: Gower, pp. 141–51.

Douglas, M. (1975), 'Deciphering a meal', in Douglas (ed.), *Implicit Meanings*, London: Routledge and Kegan Paul, pp. 249–75.

—— (1977), 'Structures of gastronomy', in *The Future and the Past: Annual Report of the Russell Sage Foundation*, New York: Russell Sage Foundation, pp. 55–81.

—— (1982a) [1973], 'Food as a system of communication', in Douglas (ed.), *In the Active Voice*, London: Routledge and Kegan Paul, pp. 82–104.

—— (1982b) [1974], 'Food as an art form', in Douglas (ed.), *In the Active Voice*, London: Routledge and Kegan Paul, pp. 105–13.

—— (1982c) [1981], 'Good taste: review of Pierre Bourdieu, *La Distinction*', in Douglas (ed.), *In the Active Voice*, London: Routledge and Kegan Paul, pp. 125–34.

—— (ed.) (1982d), *Essays in the Sociology of Perception*, London: Routledge and Kegan Paul.

—— (1984), 'Standard social uses of food', in Douglas (ed.), *Food in the Social Order: Studies of Food and Festivities in Three American Communities*, New York: Russell Sage Foundation, pp. 18–39.

Douglas, M. and Gross, J. (1981), 'Food and culture: measuring the intricacy of rule systems', *Social Science Information*, 20, 1, pp. 1–35.

Driver, C. (1983), *The British at Table 1940–1980*, London: Chatto and Windus.

Dwyer, J. T., Mayer, L. D. V. H., Dowd, K., Kandel, R. F. and Mayer, J. (1974), 'The new vegetarians: the natural high?', *Journal of the American Dietetic Association*, 65, pp. 529–53.

Edwards, J. S. A. (1993), 'Employee feeding – an overview', *International Journal of Contemporary Hospitality Management*, 5, 5, pp. 19–22.

Elias, N. (1978), *The Civilizing Process, Volume 1: The History of Manners*, Oxford: Basil Blackwell.

Ellis, R. (1983), 'The way to a man's heart: food in the violent home', in Murcott, A. (ed.), *The Sociology of Food and Eating*, Farnborough: Gower, pp. 164–71.

Elsey, A. (1980), *Battered Women: An Appraisal of Social Policy*, unpublished M.Sc. thesis, Cranfield Institute of Technology, UK.

Erlichman, J. (1993), 'Holding the pursestrings', *The Guardian*, 21 December, p. 6.

Farb, P. and Armelagos, G. (1980), *Consuming Passions: The Anthropology of Eating*, Boston: Houghton-Mifflin.

Fiddes, N. (1991), *Meat: A Natural Symbol*, London: Routledge.

Fieldhouse, P. (1986), *Food and Nutrition: Customs and Culture*, London: Croom Helm.

Finkelstein, J. (1989), *Dining Out: A Sociology of Modern Manners*, Cambridge: Polity.

Firth, R. (1973), *Symbols: Private and Public*, London: George Allen and Unwin.

Fischler, C. (1980), 'Food habits, social change and the nature/culture dilemma', *Social Science Information*, 19, 6, pp. 937–53.

—— (1986), 'Learned versus "spontaneous" dietetics: French mothers' views of what children should eat', *Social Science Information*, 25, 4, pp. 945–6.

—— (1988a), 'Food, self and identity', *Social Science Information*, 27, 2, pp. 275–92.

—— (1988b), 'Cuisines and food selection', in Thomson, D. H. (ed.), *Food Acceptability*, London: Elsevier, pp. 193–206.

Gardner, K. and Wood, R. C. (1991), 'Theatricality in food service work', *International Journal of Hospitality Management*, 10, 3, pp. 267–78.

Garine, I. de (1972), 'The socio-cultural aspects of nutrition', *Ecology of Food and Nutrition*, 1, 143–63.

George, S. (1976), *How the Other Half Dies*, Harmondsworth: Penguin.

Gibson, A. and Smout, T. C. (1988), 'Food and hierarchy in Scotland', in Leneman, L. (ed.), *Perspectives in Scottish Social History: Essays in honour of Rosalind Mitchison*, Aberdeen: Aberdeen University Press, pp. 33–52.

Gillespie, C. H. (1993), *Gastrosophy: A Medium for the Transmission of Professional Gastronomy*, unpublished M.Phil. thesis, University of Strathclyde, UK.

—— (1994), 'Gastrosophy and nouvelle cuisine: entreprenurial fashion and fiction', *British Food Journal*, in press.

Gofton, L. (1986), 'The rules of the table: sociological factors influencing food choice', in Ritson, C., Gofton., L. and McKenzie, J. (eds), *The Food Consumer*, New York: John Wiley, pp. 127–53.

—— (1989), 'Sociology and food consumption', *British Food Journal*, 91, 1, pp. 25–31.

Goode, J., Theophano, J. and Curtis, K. (1984), 'A framework for the analysis of continuity and change in shared sociocultural rules for food use: the Italian-American pattern', in Keller Brown, L. and Mussell, K. (eds), *Ethnic and Regional Foodways in the United States: the Performance of Group Identity*, Knoxville: University of Tennessee Press, pp. 66–86.

Goody, J. (1982), *Cooking, Cuisine and Class*, Cambridge: Cambridge University Press.

Harris, M. (1986), *Good to Eat: Riddles of Food and Culture*, London: George Allen and Unwin.

—— (1987), 'Foodways: historical overview and theoretical prolegomenon', in Harris, M. and Ross, E. B. (eds), *Food and Evolution: Towards a Theory of Human Food Habits*, Philadelphia: Temple University Press, pp. 57–90.

Harris, M. and Ross, E. B. (1978), 'How beef became king', *Psychology Today*, 12, 5, pp. 88–94.

Hazan, M. (1981), *The Classic Italian Cookbook*, London: Macmillan.

Hornsby-Smith, M. P. (1984), 'Sociological aspects of food behaviour: an analysis of recent trends in Britain', *Journal of Consumer Studies and Home Economics*, 8, pp. 199–216.

Hughes, M. L. (1977), 'Regional food preferences within Britain's catering industry', *HCIMA Review*, 2, 2, pp. 78–88.

Jary, D. and Jary, J. (1991), *Collins Dictionary of Sociology*, London: HarperCollins.

Jenkins, K. (1991), *Re-thinking History*, London: Routledge.

Jerome, N. W. (1980), 'Diet and acculturation: the case of Black American migrants', in Jerome, N. W., Kandel, R. F. and Pelto, G. (eds), *Nutritional Anthropology*, New York: Redgrave Publishing, pp. 275–325.

Kandel, R. F. and Pelto, G. (1980), 'The health food movement: social revitalization or alternative health maintenance system?', in Jerome, N. W., Kendel, R. F. and Pelto, G. (eds), *Nutritional Anthropology*, New York: Redgrave Publishing, pp. 327–63.

Kerr, N. and Charles, N. (1986), 'Servers and providers: the distribution of food within the family', *Sociology*, 34, 1, pp. 115–57.

Knutson, A. L. (1965), *The Individual, Society and Health Behavior*, New York: Russell Sage Foundation.

Kottak, C. P. (1978), 'Ritual at McDonald's', *Natural History Magazine*, 87, 1, pp. 75–82.

Kraig, B. (1988), 'The American hot dog: standardised taste and regional variations', in Jaine, T. (ed.), *Taste: Oxford Symposium on Food and Cookery, 1988*, London: Prospect Books, pp. 108–13.

Leach, E. (1974), *Lévi-Strauss*, London: Fontana.

Lehrer, A. (1969), 'Semantic cuisine', *Journal of Linguistics*, 5, pp. 39–55.

——— (1972), 'Cooking vocabularies and the culinary triangle of Lévi-Strauss', *Anthropological Linguistics*, 14, 5, pp. 155–71.

Lévi-Strauss, C. (1965), 'The Culinary Triangle', *Partisan Review*, 33, pp. 586–95.

McKenzie, J. (1967), *Food Choice and Price: A Supplementary Report to The British Eating Out*, Glasgow: National Catering Inquiry.

McKie, L. J. and Wood, R. C. (1991), 'Dietary information and dietary beliefs and practices amongst working-class women in north-east England', *British Food Journal*, 93, 4, pp. 25–8.

McKie, L. J., Wood, R. C. and Gregory, S. (1993), 'Women defining health: food, diet and body image', *Health Education Research*, 8, 1, pp. 35–41.

Mars, G. and Nicod, M. (1984), *The World of Waiters*, London: George Allen and Unwin.

Mars, V. (1983), 'Spaghetti – but not on toast! Italian food in London', in *Food in Motion: Proceedings of the Oxford Symposium on Food and Cooking 1983*, London: Prospect Books, pp. 144–9.

Marshall, J. (1991), 'The family that no longer eats together', *The Independent*, 16 February, p. 35.

Mazurkiewicz, R. (1983), 'Gender and social consumption', *The Service Industries Journal*, 3, 1, pp. 49–62.

Mennell, S. (1985), *All Manners of Food: Eating and Taste in England and France from the Middle Ages to the Present*, Oxford: Basil Blackwell.

Mennell, S., Murcott, A. and van Otterloo, A. (1992), *The Sociology of Food: Eating, Diet and Culture*, London: Sage.

Mercer, K. (1977), 'Some phenomena and limitations on the understanding of why we eat', *HCIMA Review*, 2, 2, pp. 65–75.

Merton, R. K. (1949), *Social Theory and Social Structure*, Glencoe: Free Press (3rd edn, 1968).

Mintz, S. (1985), *Sweetness and Power: The Place of Sugar in Modern History*, London: Viking.

Murcott, A. (1982), 'On the social significance of the "cooked dinner" in South Wales', *Social Science Information*, 21, 4/5, pp. 677–96.

—— (ed.) (1983a), *The Sociology of Food and Eating*, Farnborough: Gower.

—— (1983b), 'Introduction', in Murcott (ed.), *The Sociology of Food and Eating*, Farnborough: Gower.

—— (1986a), 'You are what you eat: explorations of anthropological factors influencing food choice', in Ritson, C., Gofton, L. and McKenzie, J. (eds), *The Food Consumer*, New York: John Wiley, pp. 107–25.

—— (1986b), 'Review of S. Mennell, *All Manners of Food: Eating and Taste in England and France from the Middle Ages to the Present*', *Sociology*, 20, 4, pp. 645–6.

—— (1988), 'Sociological and social anthropological approaches to food and eating', *World Review of Nutrition and Dietetics*, 55, pp. 1–40.

National Catering Inquiry (1966), *The British Eating Out*, Glasgow: National Catering Inquiry.

National Westminster Bank (1991), *Industry Brief: Fast Food Outlets*, London: National Westminster Bank.

Norman, J. (1992), 'Too many cooks', *Weekend Guardian*, 15–16 April, p. 14.

Passariello, P. (1990), 'Anomalies, analogies and sacred profanities: Mary Douglas on food and culture 1957–1989', *Food and Foodways*, 4, 1, pp. 53–71.

Pill, R. (1983), 'An apple a day . . . some reflections on working-class mothers' views on food and health', in Murcott, A. (ed.), *The Sociology of Food and Eating*, Farnborough: Gower, pp. 117–27.

Pill, R. and Parry, O. (1989), 'Making changes – women, food and families', *Health Education Journal*, 48, 2, pp. 51–4.

Price, S. (1993), 'Pizza home delivery boom fails to find profits', *Caterer and Hotelkeeper*, 6 May, p. 12.

Reiter, E. (1991), *Making Fast Food: From the Frying Pan into the Fryer*, Montreal: McGill Queen's University Press.

Reynolds, P. C. (1993), 'Food and tourism: towards an understanding of sustainable culture', *Journal of Sustainable Tourism*, 1, 1, pp. 48–55.

Riley, M. J. (1984), 'Hotels and group identity', *Tourism Management*, 5, 2, pp. 102–9.

Ritzer, G. (1993), *The McDonaldization of Society*, Thousand Oaks: Pine Forge Press.

Rojek, C. (1985), *Capitalism and Leisure Theory*, London: Tavistock.

—— (ed.) (1989), *Leisure for Leisure: Critical Essays*, London: Macmillan.

Saunders, C. (1981), *Social Stigma of Occupations*, Farnborough: Gower.

Seymour, D. (1983), 'The social functions of the meal', *International Journal of Hospitality Management*, 2, 1, pp. 3–7.

Sturrock, J. (1986), *Structuralism*, London: Paladin.

Thomas, J. (1980), 'The relation between knowledge about food and nutrition and food choice', in Turner, M. (ed.), *Nutrition and Lifestyles*, London: Applied Science Publishers, pp. 157–67.

—— (1982), 'Food habits of the majority: evolution of the current UK pattern', *Proceedings of the Nutrition Society*, 41, pp. 211–28.

Tomlinson, M. and Warde, A. (1993), 'Social class and change in eating habits', *British Food Journal*, 95, 1, pp. 3–10.

Twigg, J. (1983), 'Vegetarianism and the meanings of meat', in Murcott, A. (ed.), *The Sociology of Food and Eating*, Farnborough: Gower, pp. 18–30.

Urry, J. (1990), *The Tourist Gaze*, London: Sage.

Visser, M. (1986), *Much Depends on Dinner*, London: Penguin.

—— (1992), *The Rituals of Dinner*, London: Viking.

Warde, A. (1994), 'Review of S. Mennell, A. Murcott and A. van Otterloo, *The Sociology of Food: Eating, Diet and Culture*', *Sociology*, 28, 1, pp. 350–1.

Whiteman, J. (1966), 'The function of food in society', *Nutrition*, 20, pp. 4–8.

Wilson, G. (1989), 'Family food systems: preventive health and dietary change: a policy to increase the health divide', *Journal of Social Policy*, 18, 2, pp. 167–85.

Wood, A. (1989), 'Lager clout', *Caterer and Hotelkeeper*, 14 September, pp. 49–55.

Wood, R .C. (1990), 'Gender, sociology, food consumption and the hospitality industry', *British Food Journal*, 92, 6, pp. 3–5.

—— (1991), 'The shock of the new: a sociology of nouvelle cuisine', *Journal of Consumer Studies and Home Economics*, 15, 4, pp. 327–38.

—— (1992a), *Working in Hotels and Catering*, London: Routledge.

—— (1992b), 'Dining out in the urban context', *British Food Journal*, 94, 9, pp. 3–5.

—— (1992c), 'Gender and trends in dining out', *Nutrition and Food Science*, September/October, pp. 18–21.

—— (1994), 'Hotel culture and social control', *Annals of Tourism Research*, 21, 1, pp. 65–80.

# Index